Improvisation, 2nd Edition:

Use What You Know—
Make Up What You Don't!

Improvisational Activities
for the Classroom

by
Brad Newton

Gifted Psychology Press, Inc.

Improvisation, 2nd Edition: Use What You Know—Make Up What You Don't!

Published by
Gifted Psychology Press, Inc.
P.O. Box 5057
Scottsdale, AZ 85261

Formerly Ohio Psychology Press
P.O. Box 90095
Dayton, OH 45490

Printed and bound in the United States of America

04 03 02 01 00 99   6 5 4 3 2

Library of Congress Cataloging-in-Publication Data

Newton, Brad.
     Improvisation: use what you know--make up what you don't!:
improvisational activities for the classroom/by Brad Newton. --
2nd ed.
          p.   cm.
     Includes bibliographical references.
     ISBN 0-910707-31-6
     1. Educational games. 2. Improvisation (Acting) 3. Activity
programs in education. I. Title.
LB1029.G3N49 1999
371.39'7--dc21
                                        98-48837
                                           CIP

Acknowledgements

I wish to acknowledge the members of the improvisational comedy troupe, Kidprov, for their years of hard work in the field of educational improvisation. The years that I've spent with them have been a blessing, an inspiration and a great way to earn a living. Special thanks go to Kidprov members Marc Atwood, Valarie Atwood, Bob Barraza and Shawn Patrello for their help in shooting the pictures for this book.

I would also like to extend my humble appreciation to Viola Spolin, the mother of the improvisational game. Without her, all this would never have been.

All my love and a heart-felt "thank you" to my family who did everything from typing to editing to deliveries. But thanks most of all for allowing me the alone-time needed to finish this project.

Finally, I want to express my gratitude to all of my ex-students and to all of those students and teachers who have been part of the Kidprov experience. Your hungry minds and creative souls are my daily inspiration.

Table of Contents

Warm-Ups

The Improv Games

Game Correlations to Educational Objectives

Listening/Speaking

<u>Purpose</u> (rhymes, songs, gaining information, solving problems)
Letter Point, Connections, Poetry Corner, Da Do Ron Ron, Professor, Story Time
<u>Critical Listening</u> (interpreting, analyzing, distinguishing, understanding)
Connections, Spellmaster, Professor, Naive Expert, Syllabuild
<u>Appreciation</u>
All activities
<u>Audiences</u> (suitable vocabulary, communication, directions, clarification, dramatic interpretation)
All activities

Reading

<u>Word Identification</u> (phonics, grammar, context)
Beep, Spellmaster, Professor, Story Time
<u>Structural Analysis</u> (root words, prefixes, suffixes)
Beep, Spellmaster, Professor, Story Time, (X) Word Sentences
<u>Vocabulary Development</u> (listening, drawing on experience)
Letter Point, Connections, Word Wide Web, What Are You Doing? Professor, Spellmaster, Story Time, Syllabuild
<u>Comprehension</u> (cause/effect, main idea, summary, inferences, similarities/differences)
Beep, Machine, Clay Play, Justify the Object, Zig!Zag!Zog!, Give and Take, Commercial, Top That!, Happy Birthday, Letter Point, Connections, Word Wide Web, 10 Steps, Doors, Taxi, Professor, Spellmaster, Story Time, Morph, Punch Line, Take Me to Your Leader
<u>Literary Response</u> (interpretations, logical support, connections, compare/contrast)
Commercial, Story Time, Poetry Corner, Da Do Ron Ron
<u>Text Structure/Concepts</u> (logic, literary forms, analyzing characters/plot, point-of-view)
Circle Games, Story Time, (X) Word Sentences
<u>Inquiry/Research</u> (questioning strategies, drawing conclusions, summarizing from sources)
Connections, Professor, Take Me to Your Leader, Naive Expert, Syllabuild

Writing

<u>Purpose</u> (types of writing)
10 Steps, Professor, Spellmaster, Story Time, Punch Line, Da Do Ron Ron, Poetry Corner
<u>Spelling</u>
Beep, Reading Warm-ups, 1-20, Spellmaster
<u>Grammar</u>
Syllable Sing, Circle Games, Professor, Spellmaster, Story Time, (X) Word Sentences, Sullabuild, Naive Expert
<u>Writing Processes</u> (pre-writing)
Connections, Word Wide Web, Circle Games, Professor, Story Time
<u>Connections</u> (collaboration)
Circle Games, Professor, Spellmaster, Story Time, Siamese Scene

Other Areas of Instruction

The disciplines of Social Studies and Science as well as other areas of instruction can be equally served through the previously mentioned objectives. Specific Math connections are made throughout the book on a game-by game basis.

Improvisation - The Abstract

Two wigs walk into a restaurant. The waitress says, "I'm sorry, we don't serve wigs here." And the wigs reply, "..."
Create the punch line of the joke—RIGHT NOW!

You are handed a four foot long cardboard shipping tube. What else could this be? What could it be used for? What else does it look like?
I need a response—RIGHT NOW!

Hey, what are you doing? Before you answer, please remember that you have to reply—RIGHT NOW!—with something totally different than what you are actually doing.

*   *   *   *   *   *   *   *   *   *

You have just been asked to improvise, to invent without preparation—in essence, to create in a most spontaneous manner. To most people, this off-the-top-of-your-head thinking can be intimidating, a daunting task not suitable for the slow of wit (wit-challenged, dim-witted, whim-ditted). But after presenting six years worth of improvisational comedy shows and workshops to over 250,000 teachers and students, I can safely say that these timid reactions are more fear than fact.

In reality, everyone improvises. Every day. Every hour. Every moment. The "scripts" of our lives are only a loose construct, subject to continual re-vision (re-vision: to look at again). It is our daily task to make sense of this shifting, morphing life-scape and maximize the human content that lies within the limits of its borders. Even the greatest of painters works within a limited area—the canvas. Our lives, each representing our own living canvas, contain distinct borders, boundaries and potentials. Improvisation can aid us in realizing and maximizing our potential by teaching us to respect our boundaries without sacrificing the creativity, the fun and the control.

Throughout history, boundaries have held an undeserved reputation, viewed as the "bars on the cage." Yet it is precisely these boundaries that can focus our efforts, helping to define the need, the process and the outcome (product). Cicero once penned that to be completely free, one must become subserviant to a set of laws. Freedom is the result of accepting one's limitations.

If this sounds paradoxical, it's because it is. To control a herd of wild horses, you need to make sure that they have plenty of room to roam. To harness creative energy, you must make sure that the mind converges its divergence. Dr. Mihaly Csikszentmihalyi, in his book, Flow, speaks of complexity as the paradoxical combination of differentiation (uniqueness) and integration (union). The conjunction of these polar tendencies is the vital element of the improvisational experience. The creative participants take their multiple points of view (differentiation) and, together, mold them into a unified whole (integration). Dr. Csikszentmihalyi identifies this unification as the key to mental growth.

So, what allows us to access this diverse array of data which resides in our billions and billions of neural storage closets? And more so, what allows us to access this particular information at a high, higher, and highest rate of speed?

Accessibility and speed of retrieval are two of the most vital issues in the process of learning. Learning, when truly implemented, creates a web of interrelated particulates, in which one idea connects, however obliquely, to another. This allows for the accessibility. Constantly exercising these accessible connections induces a faster rate of access. Neural pathways created and maintained in this manner not only give us the ability to take rambling journeys of remembrance, but also enable us to possess creative insight. For improvisation, it is instantly-accessed creative insight that resides at Ground-Zero.

In improvisation, the simple act of remembering becomes the foundation of creativity. Improv causes us to hop the curbs of our neural highways and explore "off road" thinking, stretching our accessibility. No 4-wheel-drive vehicles are needed here, just a spirit of adventure (motivation and enthusiasm), a full tank of gas (your brain and your attention) and a few road markers (rules to play by) that allow us to create new connections that not only reinforce what has already been learned, but grant the power of ideation—the essence of creative thinking.

Although there are many techniques that stimulate "off road" thinking—Edward De Bono's Lateral Thinking® is one, Tony Buzan's Mind-Mapping® is another—most of these techniques address a specific "muscle" of the brain or a specific type of creative process and fail to establish an "aerobic" foundation that one's creativity can build upon. In contrast, the practice of improvisation produces a systemic effect, increasing creative flexibility, stamina and speed by engaging all of the mental and emotional faculties, as well as the Multiple Intelligences in a risk-free, accepting atmosphere. It is an atmosphere where all that is done and said is both permanent and transitory, where actions and speech do not carry the stigma of "dire consequence." Each action taken and each word spoken is but a step in a larger process of developing creative potential.

The most significant consequence of the improvisational experience is change— change precipitated by continual integration. Dr. Csikszentmihalyi writes, "There are two main strategies we can adopt to improve the quality of life. The first is to try making external conditions match our goals. The second is to change how we experience external conditions to make them fit our goals better." Improvisation immerses us into a process-centered environment where the goal is the process. It is essential for the participant to justify and integrate the external conditions to promote the improvisational process and in essence, to effect change.

Through integration, improvisation becomes a cumulative process. Within its structure, participants can safely practice life skills, combining the ideas and the decisions of self and others into an ever-changing new reality that always bears close scrutiny, that always contains a kernel of liveable/learnable truth. Improv makes us aware—in real time —of our decisions and our reactions on a minute-by-minute basis. Armed with this awareness, we are more adept at facing the "truths" of daily existence and responding to the consequences of daily decisions.

Successful improvisation can simply be represented by a participant's honest response to the moment. Although it may not always provoke laughter, improvisation, ideally, should allow the audience to identify with and revel in the honesty of the moment. To try to do improvisation is oxymoronic. Victor Frankl, in his book, Man's Search for Meaning, sums it up best: "Don't aim at success—the more you aim at it and make it a target, the more you are going to miss it. For success, like happiness, cannot be pursued; it must ensue...as the unintended side-effect of one's personal dedication to a course greater than oneself." With improvisation, especially when employed by the classroom teacher, learning becomes the intended by-product of the students' activities.

Most importantly, improvisation is FUN. In his book, Flow, Dr. Csikszentmihalyi aptly reveals the "why" behind improvisation's immense appeal when he describes the various components of an enjoyable experience. Dr. Csikszentmihalyi states that an enjoyable experience:

1. Is challenging.
2. Demands concentration.
3. Has clear goals.
4. Provides immediate feedback.
5. Removes from awareness the worries and frustrations of everyday life.
6. Allows participants to exercise control over their actions.
7. Allows action and awareness to merge.
8. Promotes the loss of self-consciousness.
9. Is an end in itself.

The challenges proffered by improvisation meet each of us at our own level, yet improv still insists upon equality in all ideas, no matter the age, the status or the IQ of the creator. With the freedom that this equality engenders, fun easily takes root and blossoms into a fruit-bearing plant ready for a bountiful harvest of laughter and learning.

In conclusion, improvisation attempts to unite:
> the internal and the external
> the convergent and the divergent
> the emotions and the intellect
> integration and differentiation
> you and me

into a meaningful whole without sacrificing the uniqueness of each. To again quote from Flow, by Dr. Csikszentmihalyi, improvisation enhances "the ability to find rewards in the events of the moment."

I hope you find the moments you spend with this book rewarding.

Improvisation - The Concrete
(as opposed to abstract)
The Benefits of Improvisation

Theory only holds true if it proves itself in practice. The following tangible benefits of improvisation have been observed over the past 15 years in both long-term and short-term scenarios.

Self-confidence
Imagine standing in front of a group of your peers without a clue of what you'll say. Improvisation establishes a risk-free environment that encourages risk-taking through acceptance and support while providing the practice needed for self-confidence.

Fun
How can a teacher justify "fun" in the classroom? Well, according to brain-based research, information "sticks" better when the learning is fun. Fun is inherent in improvisation. All one needs to do is add students.

Creativity
Improv games are constructed in such a manner that creativity becomes a natural by-product of the activity. Improvisation encourages creativity through the speed of response (go with that first thought!) and the complexity of response (the justification of two conflicting ideas) in a constantly morphing environment.

Complex Thinking
The integration of diverse points of view produces an increasingly complex scenario. In improv, the students' goal is to make sense of the chaos. In chaos resides possibilities. Students learn to see and react to situations from novel viewpoints as the unpredictable improvisations of others unfolds.

Critical Thinking
Although improv demands that students think "off the tops of their heads," a cognitive strata of critical analysis exists just under the surface of "right now!" Following the structure of the activity, analyzing the ideas of others and relating one's own ideas to those of others all require critical thinking.

Problem-Solving
Life is a continuous exercise in problem-solving. Improvisation creates a safe haven for students to practice problem-solving without suffering "permanent" consequences. Many of the improv games employ the students' problem-solving powers of observation, examination, inference, justification and analogy.

Structure

Form liberates. Although the improvisational games are a series of loose constructs, they supply students with targets for their creative energies. The artist's canvas, the musician's scale, the child's sandbox and the rules of improvisation all help to define the method, the medium, the message and, ultimately, the madness of the product.

Decision-Making

Like problem-solving, improv provides students with the opportunity to experiment making decisions. The cause-and-effect of their decisions can be studied and reviewed. Armed with this insight, students have a better chance of making the "right" decisions in life.

Sense of Humor

One of the most treasured personality traits is a sense of humor. The rules of the improv games are structured to produce humorous moments. As part of the improvisational process, both as actors and as audience members, students develop a healthy appreciation for what is funny.

Writing

Speaking preceeds writing. Many of the improv games demand good sentence structure, narrative skills, a healthy vocabulary and logic. As these skills are nurtured through verbalization, they are easily transferred to the development of prose.

Empathy

Accepting and flexibly integrating the ideas of another are the essentials of improvisation. In improv, there is no such thing as "denial." By consistently practicing acceptance and integration, not only will the students become more empathetic but they will become more accepting of their own ideas (see self-confidence).

Memory

Memory involves making connections, new information linking to that which is already in place. Improvisation mobilizes knowledge, facts and information, effectively weaving the new into the established to form an original tapestry.

The Do's of Improvisation
(to be shared with students)

Do trust your first instinct or thought and commit to it. There is no wrong in improvisation (as long as you follow the rules of the game).

Do listen. It's up to you to respond!

Do accept everything on stage. To deny what another says or does will disrupt the flow and will limit the chances to practice problem solving.

Do be considerate of other players. Everyone has the right to contribute in improvisation.

Do speak to be heard. Believe in what you have to say.

Do relax. Brains work more efficiently when they aren't stressed out.

Do show respect to your audience. Relying on vulgarities is a non-creative cop-out (See first "Do").

Do have FUN. It's what improvisation is all about.

Note to the Teacher on
Audience Suggestions

Audience suggestions are the backbone of the improvisational technique. Ideas given by audience members should be readily accepted without question. At some point, though, the class/audience may get into a rut, constantly throwing out mundane or repetitive suggestions. It is up to the teacher to push the students beyond the tried and true (and boring) ideas into the realm of the creative. In this way, the divergency and freshness of the activities remain intact.

Players usually begin a presentation by soliciting a suggestion from the audience. The players may choose one of the categories below (followed by an example) or create one of their own:

Active Activity (Bowling)
Historical Person (Lincoln)
Non-Geographical Locale (Kitchen)
Emotion (Anger)
Nationality (Italian)
Occupation (Astronaut)
Cartoon Character (Popeye)
Verb (Wrestling)
Noun (UFO)

Animal (Zebra)
Place (Cleveland)
Appliance (Toaster)
School Subject (Lunch)
Commercial Product (Eggos)
Something You Love To Do
(Go on vacation)
Something You Hate To Do
(Grade papers)

Once a suggestion is received from the audience, it becomes the driving force (main idea) behind the improvisational activity. The players are always responsible for justifying the suggestion. They may approach the topic from any angle. For example, the suggestion of "Astronaut" may lead to a scene in which a young boy dreams of space travel, or it may inspire a skit dealing with eating donuts in space. Overall, it is important to promote a divergent attitude toward audience suggestions.

Many students will offer suggestions that relate to their immediate surroundings (example: chair, blackboard, pencil, etc.). When giving suggestions, the students need to move their minds outside of their environment and dig for creative, non-standard ideas. Of course, suggestions should always be in good taste. Even though improvisation denotes freedom of expression, the teacher's rules and expectations of classroom conduct should always be followed.

Warm-up Activities
"WUPS"

Warm-up activities help build strong students in four ways.

1. When student energy is low, "WUPS" can energize them and get them ready to learn.

2. The students have just returned from recess and are all wound up. "WUPS" can refocus their energies into a more constructive mode, thereby preparing them to learn.

3. "WUPS" are the first step in performing successful improvisation. They teach students to think quickly, to think divergently, to focus their attention and to lose their stage fright.

4. When curriculum is folded into the mix, "WUPS" are excellent activities to teach, extend and reinforce lessons.

But please remember...Fun First!

PANTOMIME

A student adept at **PANTOMIME** communicates more fluently with fellow actors and the audience. This is why **PANTOMIME** is an integral part of improvisation. To learn the art of mime, it is important to start the student with a simple activity, such as opening a door. The student analyzes the action, looking at each step in the overall process.

PANTOMIME can be practiced in many spare moments. Playground games can be mimed rather than actually played. Car doors are opened and closed as the student "enters" his desk. **PANTOMIME** gives the student a new awareness of his physical relationship to the environment. More thought is given to the body's actions in space, and he is able to communicate more efficiently. Spatial intelligence as well as the kinesthetic sense are enhanced.

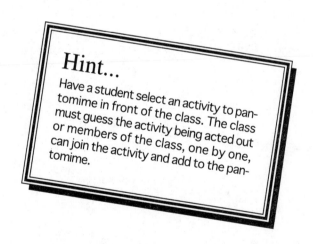

Hint...

Have a student select an activity to pantomime in front of the class. The class must guess the activity being acted out or members of the class, one by one, can join the activity and add to the pantomime.

Refer to:
Machine, Clay Play, 10 Steps, Taxi, Freeze, Morph, What Are You Doing?, Just Do It!, All Scene Games

EMOTIONAL PARADE

EMOTIONAL PARADE gives students practice in portraying various emotions, both verbally and physically. The class is evenly divided and placed in two lines that are facing each other. The student at the front of one line is given an emotion to portray by a member of the other line. She begins to slowly walk down between the two lines while portraying her emotion. After finishing her parade, she takes her place at the end of the line in which she started. The person at the front of the other line then begins his emotional walk, as he is given a different emotion to portray. Paraders alternate from line to line. Walking between members of a discerning audience gives the students experience in being closely observed by a group while in character.

EMOTIONAL PARADE is a relatively risk-free way to soothe any feelings of stage fright. Once the group is comfortable with this activity, a more advanced version can be introduced. As a player parades down the aisle, different members of the group shout out various emotions. The parader must instantly change to the emotion that is called for. In the advanced version, it is likely that class members will shout out emotions at a break-neck pace. You may want to demonstrate the pacing during a few trial runs. Three or four emotional changes during the span of an average walk is sufficient.

The suggestions of emotions are a key component in later activities. This is a good way to compile a diverse repertoire of emotions.

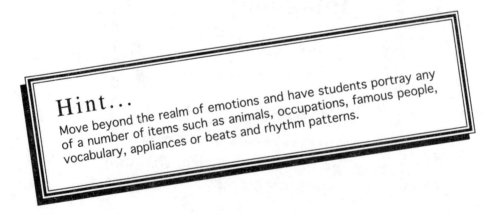

Hint...
Move beyond the realm of emotions and have students portray any of a number of items such as animals, occupations, famous people, vocabulary, appliances or beats and rhythm patterns.

Refer to:
Mirror, Group VCR, Commercial, Contagious Emotion, What Are You Doing?

CLAY PLAY

CLAY PLAY is a non-verbal activity that enhances a student's ability to show what is happening rather than tell what is happening. It relies upon the pantomiming of the critical attributes of an object. A circle of four to ten students is formed. The teacher then hands one of the students a piece of imaginary clay. The student molds the clay into some object and demonstrates that object. No words are to be spoken, although an occasional sound effect can be used to punctuate the demonstration. The group then guesses what was formed, thus giving the "sculptor" immediate feedback. If the class guesses wrong, the student must reapproach the problem from a different direction, adding more detail to the demonstation. When correctly guessed, the clay is passed on to the next student, who molds a new object. In this manner, the clay continues around the circle.

This book includes, free of charge, your own glob of imaginary clay!

Imaginary clay
goes here.

Please be sure to return the clay
to its proper place after every use!

Refer to:
Pass the Hat, Justify the Object, Happy Birthday, What Are You Doing?, Morph, Just Do It!

MACHINE

"What you can do, or dream you can, begin it; boldness has genius, power and magic in it."

Goethe

MACHINE promotes the spirit of cooperation and mutual observation in a group of students while giving practice in pantomime skills. Four to six students create a human machine, each person representing a piece of the machinery. With the group in a straight line, the end student begins a machine-like motion. After a few seconds, the next student integrates his own mechanical motion with the movement of the first. The rest of the players add their motions until the entire group is moving as a "machine." The speed of the machine can be increased or decreased by any of the members of the group. Speed changes must be made gradually. The activity terminates with the machine slowly grinding to a halt. Sounds can also be incorporated into the machine. To increase the difficulty of **MACHINE**, a circle can be formed where the first and last pieces of the machine must mesh, forming a seamless flow of mechanical energy.

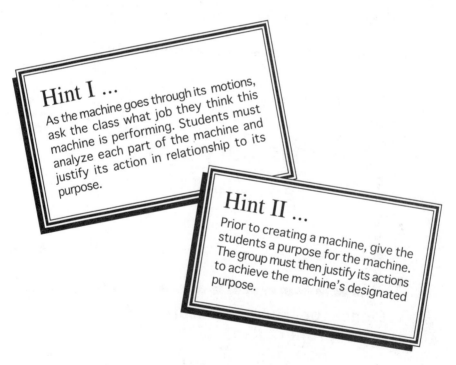

Hint I ...

As the machine goes through its motions, ask the class what job they think this machine is performing. Students must analyze each part of the machine and justify its action in relationship to its purpose.

Hint II ...

Prior to creating a machine, give the students a purpose for the machine. The group must then justify its actions to achieve the machine's designated purpose.

Refer to:
Pantomime, Give and Take, Fraction Action, Freeze

BEEP

BEEP is a warm-up activity that instantly raises the energy level of the classroom while creating an atmosphere of teamwork and cooperation. A group of students (5-20) form a circle tight enough to have their elbows touching. A student is designated to start the activity by looking to the student to her right and saying "BEEP!" Upon hearing this, the second student immediately turns to his right and says "BEEP." In this manner, the word "BEEP" is passed around the circle. Initially, the flow of the "BEEP" will be choppy, but as it continues around the circle two or three times, the stream of "BEEPS" will become a continuous flow of energized sound. Emphasis is placed on the energy created by the activity through anticipation and teamwork. It is not intended for creative anarchistic "beeping."

Hint...

To increase the complexity and diversity of **BEEP**, have the first person in the circle start with a syllable of any word of his choice (do not tell the group). The next person in line adds the second syllable that he thinks fits, and so on. When a word is finished, the next player starts another word. Soon, words of varying syllabic length will speed around the circle. (Ex: the first player thinks of the word "elephant." He says "el." The next player in line says "ah" and the third responds with "vate." Player four begins a new word with "toe"....)

More Hints...

*Pass physical motions around the circle (clapping, etc.).
*Create patterns of physical motion (clap, stomp, snap) that go around the circle. Starting with a one-step pattern, continue to add to the number of steps in the pattern.
*Pass a multi-syllablic word around the circle one syllable at a time (tor-na-do).
*Create a number pattern (count by 2's, add 3, then subtract 1).

Refer to:
Circle Games, Professor, Spellmaster

LETTER POINT

Math Hints...

*The center person represents a number (Ex: "3") and an operation ("times"). As he points to students, he says a number ("7"). The response must be the product of the two numbers ("21"). With younger students, the sum of the two ("10") would be the response.

*Send a student out of the room. Choose a number and operation for him to represent. Bring the student back into the room and place him in the middle of the circle. Play as above and have the student attempt to guess what number and operation he represents.

LETTER POINT enhances a student's ability to react to and access information and become more fluent in ideation. A student is chosen to stand in the center of a circle of 5-10 of his peers. He then begins randomly pointing at the students in the circle. As he points to a student, he says a letter from the alphabet. The student pointed at must immediately respond with a (nice) word that begins with the given letter. Pointing continues in random fashion at a quick pace. **LETTER POINT** can also be played while students are seated at their desks. One student, who is the pointer, is mobile and moves about the room.

Hints...

*With younger students, the sound the letter makes should follow the saying of the letter ("B, buh").

*A theme (main idea) is chosen and all words must connect with that theme (adjectives, nouns, animals, food, etc.).

*From time to time, a student may be at a loss for a word. This student can be coached with clues and questions. Above all, let the student work through the thinking. It is common for other students in the circle to blurt out a word to help another who is "stuck." Remind students that you are building mental muscles here and that they should not give help unless asked.

*Letter Point Alliteration: a letter is given ("B!") and the response must be two words that start with that letter ("Big Bunny!"). Advanced students can be asked to use an adjective and a noun as the two words.

Refer to:
Professor, Spellmaster, Story Time, Tag Rhyme

Lorayne & Lucas

CONNECTIONS

CONNECTIONS allows students to practice accessing their knowledge base through associating a topic with its related parts (constituent parts). A main idea or topic is agreed upon (Ex: the farm). A student is designated as the pointer and enters the center of a circle. That student then randomly points to members of the circle. When pointed to, a student must respond with a word that somehow relates to the main idea (Ex: chicken). Once a related word is offered, it can not be repeated. The pointer quickly points around the circle in random fashion, eliciting responses. Students who give a response that is out of the ordinary may be challenged by the pointer (or other members of the circle) to justify his response. **CONNECTIONS** can be played while students are at their desks with the pointer moving about the room. By playing **CONNECTIONS**, students mobilize their knowledge of any given subject or topic by associating diverse ideas and creating new memory connections.

Hints...

*Send the pointer out of the room. A main idea is chosen. The pointer then returns, plays the game and attempts to draw conclusions as to the identity of the topic.

*For older students, two or even three main ideas can be used simultaneously. The pointer must identify multiple main ideas, mentally separating clues into the various categories.

*Reverse the game. Only the pointer knows the main idea. As he points to members of the circle, they say a word. The pointer responds with "in" if the word relates to the main idea, or "out" if the word given does not apply. It's up to the members of the circle to guess the main idea. This game leads to lots of discussion. After the main idea is correctly guessed, it is advantageous for the players to discuss how the game went.

*Odyssey of the Mind spontaneous problem prompts are intriguing to use with this game (Ex: things that are blue, things that go under other things, etc.).

Refer to:
Letter Point, Word Wide Web, Poetry Corner,
Da Do Ron Ron, Punch Line

WORD
WIDE
WEB

"If you come to a fork in the road, take it."
Yogi Berra

Hints...

*Tape record the activity and, by following the step-by-step process of the verbal web, students can critically analyze the route that their responses took as they define the inter-relatedness of ideas along the way.

*By looking at the beginning topic and the final word spoken, students can discuss the connections between the two.

WORD WIDE WEB is the physical and verbal equivalent to Mind Mapping (©Tony Buzan). As in **CONNECTIONS**, a main idea is chosen and a pointer elicits related words from members of the circle. At random times, the teacher (or leader) yells, "Freeze!" At this point, the person in the circle who gave the last response becomes the pointer, and her response becomes the new main idea. The game continues as main ideas are changed whenever "Freeze!" is called out.

Pre-Writing Hints...

*As a pre-writing strategy, **WORD WIDE WEB** pushes students outside of their own imaginations, providing new ideas to work with. Specifically, start with the main idea of conflict. Students begin relating different types of conflicts. Switch to character, then to setting, then to resolution. The number of ideas and the potential relationships between them create a number of possible narrative scenarios. You may want to switch the order of the prompts (start with character, move to resolution, etc.).

Refer to:
Letter Point, Connections, Morph, Freeze, Punch Line

READING WARM-UPS

For students to realize the importance of each word and its corresponding sounds, it is paramount that they practice the art of speaking. The following reading warm-ups focus on speaking rhythms and word inflection. With a "sound foundation" in the "essential elements" of speaking, a student becomes a more effective and more entertaining communicator.

S....L....O....W M....O....T....I....O....N R....E....A....D....I....N....G....

Students read from any prepared text in slow motion. They take care to read each syllable with the same inflection that they would use if the text was read at normal speed. It may be helpful to read the text at a normal rate first to give a basis for comparison. Dialogue from plays or comic strips can be applied to this activity to create a slow motion conversation between two or more students. (Imagine Hamlet's soliloquy in slow motion, or for that matter Green Eggs and Ham). It is the sound of the words, not the meaning, that this activity emphasizes. It truly is a "meaning-less" exercise.

SPELL READING

Students read from any prepared text by spelling each word. The rhythm and inflection of the words should remain intact. For comparison, it may help to read the sentences normally before spelling them. Advanced students may wish to hear the spelling version first and attempt to decipher what is being "spell read." Anticipate parent opposition to the advanced variation. They will never be able to spell out things in front of their kids again.

SINGING PHRASES

Students use any prepared text or list and instead of reading it, they sing it. Imagine the Gettysburg Address sung to the tune of the theme song to "Gilligan's Island," or the periodic table of the elements sung to the tune, "Stairway to Heaven." Singing is an excellent way to help students memorize information. Hey, if the Beatles had written songs about differential calculus, how many of us would now be mathematicians? **SINGING PHRASES** is a precursor to the game **MUSICAL SCENE**. Melodies may be improvised, or the students may set the words to a familiar tune. To generate a singing conversation, use a play, or even better, a comic strip as the basis for the singing.

Refer to:
All activities

SYLLABLE SING

SYLLABLE SING emphasizes listening skills. Two to four students are asked to leave the room so as to be out of earshot. The rest of the class is divided into three equal groups. A three syllable word is suggested by a class member. Each group is given one syllable of the word to sing to the tune of a familiar song (Example: "Row, Row, Row Your Boat"). All three groups sing their individual syllable at the same time in melodic unison. The absent students are then brought back into the room to attempt to decipher the three syllable word that the class is singing.

Hint...

Vary the number of syllables you use in the game according to the level of your class. Younger students find **SYLLABLE SING** a real challenge, as it helps them in defining the division of syllables. Phonics, anyone?

Refer to:
Machine, 3-Way Conversation, Da Do Ron Ron, Naive Expert, Syllabuild

GIBBERISH

GIBBERISH is spoken sound that closely resembles language but with one exception—it makes no sense. **GIBBERISH** is composed of a series of nonsense words and sounds strung together with intonation so as to simulate language. Using gibberish in an improv game lays the burden of communication on pantomime skills, yet a student with the "gift of gibber" can enhance his pantomime through the prudent use of gibberish. Listed below are warm-ups that facilitate the student's ability to use gibberish while helping students see the connection between gibberish and actual language.

1
Two students simulate a conversation in gibberish with no meaning intended or inferred. The participants focus on the sound, the rhythm and the timing of their speech. This activity also allows them to practice the give-and-take in an improvised conversation.

2
Two students converse (one in gibberish; one in English) in order to communicate specific information. The focus of this activity is on the use of inflection and rhythm to communicate. Very little pantomime should be used. Each player secretly decides upon a simple message to convey (Examples: "Button your shirt," "Let's go bowling," " Your hair's on fire!"). The first student attempts to communicate the message. The other student responds in English, communicating to the "gibberer" what he understands the message to be. This gives the "gibberer" instant feedback and allows him to alter his presentation if the message is not being received. When the message has been communicated, the second student attempts to convey a different message.

3
Two students strike up a conversation using English. At random intervals, a third student calls out either "Gibberish" or "English" and the two must immediately switch to the called style while retaining the flow of the conversation. This aids in the assimilation of normal language patterns into **GIBBERISH**. To increase the difficulty, two callers can be employed, one for each person. The possibility of a dual language conversation now exists.

Home Hint...
Tired of phone solicitors? Use some gibberish on them and the results are guaranteed!

Here's some gibberish to practice on:
"Crotubel neefoot cran dibble san deefoosa. Nost quallak ma toondy."

Refer to:
Commercial, Take Me to Your Leader, Just Do It!

EYE SCREAM

Improv is all about commitment—the commitment to an idea, the commitment to a course of action. **EYE SCREAM** is a kinesthetic activity bent on improving one's commitment. With 7-12 students formed in a circle, everyone looks at a point on the floor in the center of the circle. Everyone counts to three, slowly and in unison. On "3!" everyone looks up and stares directly at another person in the circle. There must be a commitment to one person and one person only! No wandering eyes! If the person being stared at is staring directly back, those two students scream and step out of the circle. We're talking about SCREAM! here, not scream. After the "screamers" step out, the next round begins and the game continues until there are only one or two left in the circle.

Intellectual? No. Important? Yes. **EYE SCREAM** puts students into the position of making quick decisions and sticking to them. This activity can directly effect the success of many of the improv games described in this book, since most, if not all, improv games demand decisiveness and commitment.

Hint...
Use **EYE SCREAM** as a specific precusor to the game ZIG!ZAG!ZOG!. We have found that **EYE SCREAM's** focus on commitment dramatically elevates the students' ability to play ZIG!ZAG!ZOG!

Refer to:
All activities

ZIG!ZAG!ZOG!

ZIG!ZAG!ZOG! is a game demanding total concentration. A group of 4-8 students forms a circle large enough to allow everyone to see each other without having to turn too much. A player (designated by the group) begins as he looks at a person across the circle, makes sure to get eye contact, and says, "ZIG!" The "ZIGGER" must stand relatively still as he says, "ZIG." The person to whom the ZIG is directed (the "ZIGGEE") then looks to another person, gets eye contact, and says "ZAG!" being sure to remain still. The one who has just been "ZAGGED" (the "ZAGGEE") then gets eye contact with any member of the circle, takes one step toward him, slaps his hands together, points at the person, and says, "ZOG!" (see photo) This is all done in one simultaneous motion. Once the "ZOGGING" motion is complete, the "ZOGGER" steps back into the circle. The "ZOGGED" individual begins the cycle over by looking at another and saying "ZIG!" In this manner, the activity continues.

ZIG!ZAG!ZOG! develops listening skills and hand/eye coordination. Expect the activity to move slowly at first, but speed up after everyone becomes comfortable with the rules. Allow the groups to police themselves during competition. It is a unique way to work on group dynamics.

Later, a competitive edge may be added to this warm up. If a student makes a "ZOG!" movement while saying either "ZIG!" or "ZAG!," he is out. If he fails to make the proper hand and foot motion while "ZOGGING," he is out. The competition ceases when only two players remain.

Math Hints...

ZIG!ZAG!ZOG! can be used to practice math facts: for example, multiplication. Instead of "ZIG!," a player shouts out a one digit number ("7!") while looking at another player. That player then looks at another player and says a second one digit number("5!"). The third student, knowing the operation of multiplication is understood, then gives the product ("35!") as he performs the "ZOGGING" motion toward a member of the group who then begins a new equation. Addition would work equally well. Subtraction should be saved for when students are working on integers. Division takes some extra thinking. The first number must have many factors (so don't use prime numbers!). The second number must be a factor of the first and, of course, the third number (the "Zog") would be the quotient.

Algebra Hints...

Even algebra can't escape the power of ZIG!ZAG!ZOG! The first player says a one digit number and "X" ("5X!"). The second player then gives a multiple of the coefficient of X ("30!"). The third player "ZOGS" with the value of X ("6!"). A new equation is started by the player who has just been "ZOGGED."

Refer to:
Eye Scream, Bunny Bunny, Feeze, Tag Rhyme

"ZIG!"

"ZAG!"

"ZOG!"

More Hints...

ZIG!ZAG!ZOG! can also be applied to the spelling of three letter words, comparatives and superlatives, verb tenses and even notes in a chord.

"Zog" - Side View

BUNNY BUNNY

There are times when the serious nature of school needs a big dose of the sillies. **BUNNY BUNNY** allows students to let down their airs of "serious" and "cool" and be energized through just plain old silliness. With 7-12 students in a circle, a Main Bunny is selected. The Main Bunny puts both hands up as ears, wiggles them, and says over and over, "Bunny Bunny." The person to the immediate right of the Main Bunny is the Right-Eared Bunny, raising her right hand and wiggling only her right ear. The person to the immediate left of the Main Bunny is the Left-Eared Bunny, raising his left hand and wiggling only his left ear. Both the Left and Right-Eared Bunnies chime in with the Main Bunny repeating over and over, "Bunny Bunny". This continues for 3-5 seconds until the Main Bunny passes the Bunny to another player by pulling off his ears, putting the palms of his hands together as a pointer and, with one final hail and hearty "Bunny," pointing to another player in the circle. This person now becomes the Main Bunny, acquiring the appropriate Right and Left-Eared Bunnies. This continues randomly around the circle at a break-neck pace.

A few years ago, **BUNNY BUNNY** was being played by a group of hearing impaired fifth graders. One student named Chris signed to the teacher that he did not want to play **BUNNY BUNNY**. He had a better idea. And with that, the game of **CHICKEN CHICKEN** was born. Instead of Bunny ears, participants don Chicken wings (put thumbs in arm pits and start flapping). Right and Left-winged Chickens flank the Main Chicken. No, the players do not repeatedly say, "Chicken Chicken;" they cluck like maniac chickens ("Boc! Boc! Boc!"). Passing the chicken consists of folding the wings back and stretching out the chicken neck to the next player while giving one final loud "Boc!"

Hint...

*Have students invent their own version of **BUNNY BUNNY** by selecting various animals and creating their actions.
*For younger students, you may forgo the left and right Bunnies and just use a Main Bunny.
*This is a great game to help primary students differentiate between their left and their right.
*Besides diffusing their "cool factor," this is a great game to help high school students differentiate between their left and their right.

Refer to:
Zig!Zag!Zog!, Eye Scream, What Are You Doing?

"Bunny! Bunny! Bunny!"

"BUNNY!"

"Boc! Boc! Boc!"

"BOC!"

Anecdote

One hundred or so teachers were in the midst of a day-long staff development seminar, learning how to play and apply a multitude of improvisational activities. A dozen circles of teachers dotted the cafeteria as they all learned the nuances of **BUNNY BUNNY**. With a huff, one teacher refused to play, stating that the game was demeaning to her professional status. "A teacher should never participate in such a silly activity." Needless to say, she was allowed to "sit this one out," yet the evaluation she submitted at the end of the workshop vehemently berated **BUNNY BUNNY**, as well as many of the activities presented that day. To her, these activities had no place in her FIRST GRADE classroom.

CIRCLE GAMES

Round up the students—it's time for the **CIRCLE GAMES**. The following activities are perfect to refresh stale minds, energize drained brains and best of all, they make the bossy kids stop being so bossy! Circles can contain from 5-10 students (although 6-7 works best).

WORD ASSOCIATION

The first student in the circle says any word that comes to mind. The next student responds with his first association. The third reads to the second, and so forth around the circle. We're talking quick here. Move away from "uhhh..." and "I don't know."

CIRCLE STORY (or any type of prose for that matter)

The first four people in the circle start with "Once" "upon" "a" "time," and from there, a story develops around the circle one word at a time. No hesitating, please. Initially, stories will make absolutely minimal sense, yet as students get familiar with the game and its nuances, cohesive narratives will eventually appear.

CIRCLE POLITICS

In the same manner as **CIRCLE STORY**, students create a political speech. The speech can be totally random (do this first) or related to a specific topic ("The Environment" or "Campaign Financing").

CIRCLE BUMPER STICKER

Same rules as before, but the goal of the game is to create short, pithy bumper sticker phases. As one is completed, another begins immediately.

CIRCLE PROFESSOR

Any student in the circle can ask a question. After the question is asked, the answer immediately begins, one word at a time, with the person to the right of the asker. When the question is answered, another is instantly posed by any member of the circle.

DEAR BLABBY

A student states a fictional personal problem. The circle responds one word at a time with advice from **DEAR BLABBY**. As in **CIRCLE PROFESSOR**, the student to the right of the problem-stater begins the answer. The first two students of the answer should address the person with the problem with a "Dear _____,"....

Don't limit yourself to the mentioned topics. Other suggestions for circle work are: Poetry; Mom-isms; Rules of the Road; Directions; Big Lies; Shakespeare.

Refer to:
Beep, Professor, Spellmaster, Story Time

MIRROR

Improvisation cannot work unless the students pay attention not only to what is being said, but also to what is being done. **MIRROR** focuses on the awareness of both. Pairs of students face each other, approximately 1-2 feet apart. Both put their hands up in front of them, palms facing outward. They match up their hands, getting close without actually touching each other. One of the two students is designated to be the leader. The leader slowly (repeat, slowly) moves her hands. It is up to her partner to mirror her motions. "Switch!" is yelled at various times and the leader now becomes the follower and vice-versa. To increase the difficulty, students share the leading, the right hand always leads, the left hand always follows.

FACE MIRROR is an extension of **MIRROR** in which the leader slowly makes all sorts of odd faces for the follower to mirror. Be sure both get a chance to lead. Very goofy stuff.

But the favorite mirror activity, as well as the toughest, is **VOICE MIRROR**. The leader slowly starts speaking, and the follower must say exactly what the leader says—at the same time! Be sure students speak slowly. Try voice mirror two different ways. First have the student look at his partner while speaking. In this way, visual clues can enhance the ability to mirror the speech of the other. Next, have the students close their eyes and try to mirror the conversation through voice alone. Very difficult, but loads of fun.

MIRROR is an activity of cooperation and mutual respect. Be careful that some students don't attempt to "win" at **MIRROR** by moving too fast, thereby totally confusing the followers.

Brain-based Learning Hint...

Brain-based research says: Be sure students cross the mid-line of their body from time to time with their hands. This brings a cross-lateral movement into play, helping to integrate both hemispheres of the brain.

Refer to:
Pantomime, Machine, 3-Way Conversation,
10 Steps, Taxi, Freeze, Just Do It!

GROUP STOP
GROUP VCR

"Pay attention!" Sound familiar? **GROUP STOP** and **GROUP VCR** will assist students in focusing their attention on their surroundings. Begin **GROUP STOP** with everyone, including the teacher, walking about the room. Whenever the teacher stops, all students must immediately stop. After a few minutes of this, the teacher steps out and four students are chosen as leaders. Whenever one of the four leaders stops, everyone else must stop. **GROUP STOP** then expands to the whole class. Whenever one student stops, all must stop. After all have stopped, everyone begins moving again.

GROUP VCR begins with all sudents sitting on the floor or at their desks. The teacher stands apart from the group armed with an imaginary VCR remote control. This imaginary remote has all the standard buttons: Power on; Power off; Play; Rewind; Fast forward; Slow-motion (both forward and reverse); Mute; Pause; Eject. The remote also has the ability to change channels.

The teacher begins with "Power on!" All students stand. "Play!" starts the students moving about the room at a normal rate. The teacher then manipulates the group with the use of the remote control.

"Slow-motion!" and the class begins sloth-like movements around the room.

"Fast forward!" and the whole class starts jetting about the room. (Use this sparingly!)

"Rewind!" and students reverse their motions and begin to move backwards.

"Mute!" is self-explanatory and a teacher's favorite button!

"Power off!" stops everyone in their tracks as they instantly sit down.

"Eject!" and the whole class jumps in the air.

As the activity continues, the teacher starts changing channels. Switching to "The Sports Channel" or to "The Ballet Channel" causes the students to create movements that relate to the theme of the channel. Curriculum can be easily inserted as students must relate their actions to "The Civil War Channel" or to "The Mitosis Channel."

Refer to:
Mirror, Give and Take, Taxi, Freeze, Reruns

GIVE AND TAKE

GIVE AND TAKE is an essential warm-up because it demonstrates the need for cooperation and team work. It gives students the experience of sharing the spotlight. A group of 5-10 students forms a circle. Any student may initiate a bodily movement such as moving her arm up and down. The rest of the group imitates the action. This motion is continued by the group until another member stops the first motion and begins a second. When the members of the circle see this change, however subtle it is, they all must imitate the new movement. Players continue changing motions at random with the group following.

Since there is no prepared text in improvised scenes, it is important for the student to realize that she has a responsibility to the "flow" (see glossary) of the scene. She must know when to listen and when to respond. **GIVE AND TAKE** teaches students to slow down and observe, to take control, or to give up control when it is appropriate.

When first playing **GIVE AND TAKE**, there may be pandemonium as group members initiate motions simultaneously. This is precisely why **GIVE AND TAKE** needs to be practiced. Over a period of time, students will start to relate to the "flow," allowing every member to have a say and achieving true communication between the players.

GIVE AND TAKE can also be played with sounds or a combination of sounds and motions. It all depends on the tolerance of your neighboring teachers.

Hint...

Suggest a theme for the students to base their actions on. A theme of "outer space" would demand that all players create motions that somehow relate to outer space. Freeze the group occasionally to check for group cohesion.

Refer to:
Machine, 1-20, Mirror, Group Stop, All improv games

PASS THE HAT

"Good teaching develops students' creative abilities by unlocking their sense of wonder."

Robert Grudin

PASS THE HAT is CLAY PLAY on a concrete level. Five to six students form a circle where a hat is passed around (actually, any object will suffice). When a member receives the hat, he creates something unique out of the hat (a bowl, a hand puppet, etc.) and presents it to the group. PASS THE HAT allows for verbalization in the presentation, although each creation should take only a matter of seconds. Upon completion of the "mini-skit," the hat is relayed to another in the group. In PASS THE HAT, the key is fluency. The hat is passed until each member of the circle gets three to four chances to manipulate it. Each presentation should be unique and not a repeat of someone else's idea.

Hint Sr. ...
Keep groups small so that everyone is constantly involved.

Hint Jr. ...
Students must guess (draw conclusions) what the person is creating with the hat. The creator must use pantomime only! No talking unless it's gibberish.

Refer to:
Justify the Object, Clay Play, Morph, Freeze

1-20

1-20 demands that participants become an integral part of a team that relies solely on "feel" to achieve the goal of the game—counting from one to twenty. Five students form a tight circle with hands behind their backs and eyes fixed on a point on the floor in the center of the circle. The objective is to count from 1 to 20 in numerical order. The challenge is to count randomly within the circle, in which any member of the circle can say the next number. The rule states that if two or more players say a number at the same time, the sequence must start back at one. Sound easy?

Hint...

Some students will attempt to control the game by pointing with their feet or devising elaborate patterns. Please remind them that the fun of the game is to count totally at random.

More Hints...

*Move to counting by multiples, in patterns, prime numbers, etc.
*Use spelling words, spelling them one letter at a time. When two or more players say a letter at the same time, the word must start over.
*In the same manner, use vocabulary words, but after correctly spelling them, the group must then define them.
*Create a story this way--it could be interesting...

Refer to:
Give and Take, Add-a-Scene, All improv games

FRACTION ACTION

Fractions have never been so much fun and so easy to learn. You won't hear any whining from the students "Oh no, fractions...teacher, do we half to?" **FRACTION ACTION** moves math into the realm of the kinesthetic. Two teams of four students each take the stage, making sure to have lots of room to move. When a student stands, she is equal to the whole number "1." When a student is on her knees, she is equal to "1/2." When lying on the floor, she is equal to "0." Four students standing equal "4."

In this competition (that really doesn't address winning and losing—it just makes the game more frenetic!) each team must equal the number called out by the teacher. When the number "3" is called, each team will add up to 3 as fast as possible without injuring themselves or others.

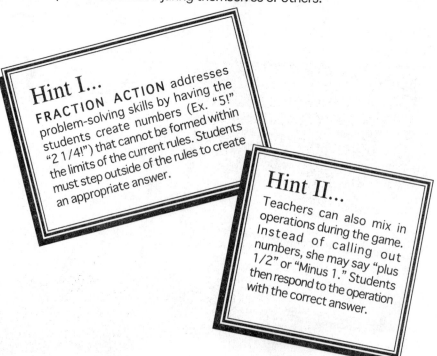

Hint I...
FRACTION ACTION addresses problem-solving skills by having the students create numbers (Ex. "5!" "2 1/4!") that cannot be formed within the limits of the current rules. Students must step outside of the rules to create an appropriate answer.

Hint II...
Teachers can also mix in operations during the game. Instead of calling out numbers, she may say "plus 1/2" or "Minus 1." Students then respond to the operation with the correct answer.

Refer to:
Syllable Sing, Give and Take, Group Stop

"4!"

"2 1/2!"

"2!"

"0!"

JUSTIFY
THE OBJECT

Justifying an object, giving specific reasons why it is involved in a scene, is an important skill in improvisation. This warm-up challenges students to justify the use of three or more unrelated objects in a scene through the use of dialogue and pantomime. This is an advanced warm-up that is best practiced after an introduction to **PASS THE HAT**.

The class suggests three objects (tire, glass of milk, pig) and a place (the moon) in which to locate them. It is up to the players (2-3) to justify the appearance of those objects in the scene (tire from an old space buggy, thirsty astronauts try to figure out how to drink milk in space, pig is a stowaway). The objects must play a part in the scene. They are not ornamental. The objects can become catalysts to the plot or the conflict.

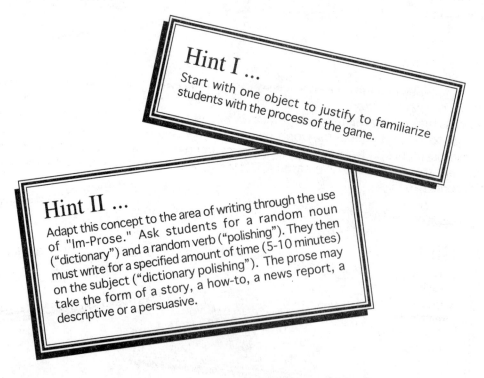

Hint I ...
Start with one object to justify to familiarize students with the process of the game.

Hint II ...
Adapt this concept to the area of writing through the use of "Im-Prose." Ask students for a random noun ("dictionary") and a random verb ("polishing"). They then must write for a specified amount of time (5-10 minutes) on the subject ("dictionary polishing"). The prose may take the form of a story, a how-to, a news report, a descriptive or a persuasive.

Refer to:
Clay Play, Pass the Hat, Morph, Freeze, Hesitation

COMMERCIAL

COMMERCIAL gives the student an opportunity to practice the art of persuasion while building self-confidence and a healthy trust in her own creativity. It is one of the few activities that relies on props. A collection of household product packaging (cereal boxes, empty cans of food, cleaning products, etc.) gives the student objects on which to base a commercial. The student blindly selects an item from the collection. A designated class member then states either "Pro" or "Con." The player begins her commercial while praising or condemning the product according to what was called.

Truth is a stretchable commodity as hyperbole, false statistics and personal opinions become the essence of the presentation. While performing the commercial, the student may want to read excerpts from the product's label, lending credibility to her presentation and arming her with more "twistable" information. The presentation should last from 30 seconds to a minute.

Upon completion of the first commercial, a second student uses the same product to create a commercial, but presents the opposite viewpoint. Emphasis is placed upon the fluency of ideas. As students become more advanced in their ability to "pitch" a product, a caller can be appointed who will, at intervals, call out "Pro" or "Con" during a presentation. The student presenting the commercial must respond to the caller by alternating her commercial between the two extremes.

When first introduced, **COMMERCIAL** is an exercise in verbal fluency. Later, it can be directed to specific persuasive techniques. To reduce the risk for beginners, discuss the critical attributes of a product before the presentation and limit the time on stage to 20 to 30 seconds. Don't be limited only to products in **COMMERCIAL**. Advertisements for historical figures, book characters, scientific theories, animals, or current trends can also be created. **COMMERCIAL** can be a way to introduce your students to debate.

Hint I ...
Collect stacks of the food section from your local paper. Have students create their own products by cutting out various words and piecing them together to form creative combos. "Dog Nog," "Hot Fudge Toothpaste" and "Cajun Moon Salsa" are but a few snips away! Use these new products as the basis for the commercials.

Hint II ...
Don't be afraid to turn this activity into a written exercise.

Refer to:
Connections, Justify the Object, Naive Expert

TOP
THAT!

TOP THAT! provides the students with a vehicle to practice give-and-take, while focusing on quick creative responses. Two students take the stage and a suggestion is solicited from the audience as to what the two will talk about (Bowling). One student starts the conversation by making a relatively braggadocious statement that refers to the topic ("My dad bowled a 300 game."). The other student then brags on himself in an attempt to top the last statement ("I bowled a 300 game with my eyes shut!"). The conversation goes back and forth, each player trying to top the other. TOP THAT! requires the participants to gradually work up to the completely outlandish lie (I own all of the bowling alleys in the universe!). The exercise ends when one player fails to top the other. Remind them that this is an exercise in self-promotion, not put-downs. Steer clear of degrading the other person.

TOP THAT! can be modified into a warm-up called COMPLIMENT. Challenge two students to out-compliment each other in the same manner of TOP THAT!

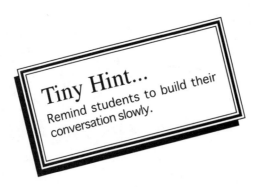

Tiny Hint...
Remind students to build their conversation slowly.

Refer to:
Yes, but..., What Are You Doing?, Taxi

YES, BUT...

Are your students an agreeable lot? Or do they constantly argue a point? Either way, **YES, BUT...** is for you. Two students are chosen to participate in the game. A theme is suggested that the players' conversation must somehow revolve around (Ex. sports). Player One begins with a question that must be answered with a "Yes/No" response ("Do you like football?"). Player Two must answer, "Yes," and then elaborate with, "but..." ("Yes, but I like baseball better."). Player One, using the information from Player Two's response, poses another "Yes/No" question ("So, then is baseball your favorite sport?"). Player Two responds ("Yes, but I find it boring at times."). Player One retorts ("So are you a boring person?"). Player Two states ("Yes, but not on the dance floor."). Player One returns with ("But you have two left feet, don't you?"). The player posing the question can put the "Yes, but" player in some awkward situations.

YES, BUT... can be altered to become the game **YES, AND...** in which the player answering the questions must elaborate upon his response.

YES, BUT... and **YES, AND...** focus on a student's ability to elaborate upon limited information through careful listening.

Refer to:
Machine, Taxi, Doors,
What Are You Doing?, Story Time

HAPPY BIRTHDAY

HAPPY BIRTHDAY, as in **CLAY PLAY**, emphasizes the ability to show rather than tell. One student enters with an imaginary box, the size and weight of her choosing. She presents the box to a second student, wishing him, "Happy birthday!" The receiver thanks the giver and proceeds to open the gift. The giver has no idea what the box contains. She has only delivered a "frame of reference" for the receiver to react to.

As the recipient opens the present, he will physically and verbally react to what he perceives its contents to be without specifically identifying it to the audience or the giver. If he perceives the gift to be a puppy, for example, he is not to say, "Oh, a puppy!" or "Golly, a dog!" He must somehow relate what the object is without naming it. In the case of the puppy, he may say, "Oh, it has such a cold nose!" or "I had better start laying out newspapers!" The critical attributes of the object are used as hints to express the object's identity.

After the receiver makes his statement, the giver attempts to guess what the object is, again giving the clue-giver immediate feedback. Wrong guesses tell the recipient to offer more information. Guesses are made until the correct one is given. They exit and the next two take the stage as the activity continues.

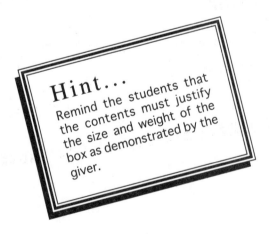

Hint...
Remind the students that the contents must justify the size and weight of the box as demonstrated by the giver.

Refer to:
Pantomime, Clay Play, Justify Object, Morph, Freeze

"To know truly is to know by causes."

Francis Bacon

How simple are the simplest tasks? How aware are we of the sequence of steps that we take in performing the easiest of our dialy routines? In **10 STEPS**, students must break a simple task (for instance, brushing one's teeth) into 10 distinct steps. The steps are recorded on the board and, after completion of the sequence, a volunteer is chosen to act out the steps exactly as they are written. Naturally, acting out only 10 steps leaves room for lots of error and equal amount of laughter.

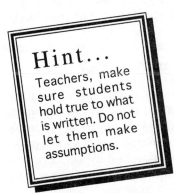

Hint...

Teachers, make sure students hold true to what is written. Do not let them make assumptions.

Two More Hints...

*10 STEPS focuses on cause and effect and its importance in proper sequencing. It dramatically demonstrates the need for observational and analytical skills.

*10 STEPS is also a great way to get students to state their ideas clearly and concisely. "Open the tube of toothpaste" can be interpreted many ways.

Refer to:
Connections, Reruns, Syllabuild, Just Do It!

3-WAY CONVERSATION

Focusing on interpersonal flexibility, multi-processing skills and plain-old listening skills, **3-WAY CONVERSATION** is not for the faint of heart. Yet after teachers experience this game, they remark that it is no different than teaching a roomful of kindergartners.

The basics? One student centered between two others must carry on a conversation with each of the other two simultaneously! The outside players choose contrasting topics to converse about. Immediately, they engage the center player in a conversation about their specific topic. The center player must move back and forth, carrying on meaningful conversation with both. The center person should be reminded that "Uh-uh," "Oh, really" and "Hmmm" are not part of engaging in the conversation. Neither is just asking questions. The center players must add to each of the conversations. Outside players must be warned not to try to dominate the conversation. This is not a competition. When the center player turns to talk to the other, he should continue talking, adding information. After a minute of this, places are switched, and a new person becomes the center player.

3-WAY CONVERSATION forces students to expand their focus, talking with one person as they "shadow listen" to another to pick up key content.

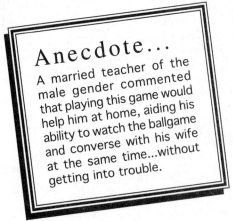

Anecdote...
A married teacher of the male gender commented that playing this game would help him at home, aiding his ability to watch the ballgame and converse with his wife at the same time...without getting into trouble.

Refer to:
Connections, Syllable Sing, Give and Take, Story Time

ADD-A-SCENE

ADD-A-SCENE combines many of the skills practiced in the previous warm-up activities. A chair is placed on center stage. A student is then asked to enter the stage and create the beginnings of a scene. It is up to this student to create a scene that somehow incorporates this chair. The chair can be used in any manner the student can imagine (lawn mower, throne, race car, etc.). After about twenty seconds, another student enters the scene. She must add an idea, emotion, conflict, etc. to the scene. The two interact as a third and possibly a fourth student enter the scene.

Once again, anyone entering the scene must affect the scene. If a player finds that he has become extraneous to the action on stage, he has every right to make an exit (including the student who started the whole scene). The flow of students exemplifies the importance of give and take. The scene continues in the manner stated until the scene's energy has run its course.

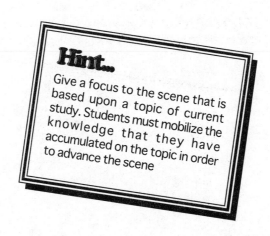

Hint...
Give a focus to the scene that is based upon a topic of current study. Students must mobilize the knowledge that they have accumulated on the topic in order to advance the scene

Refer to:
Pantomine, Taxi!, Doors, (X) Word Sentences, Rhyme Time, Contagious Emotion, Foreign Movie, Reruns

DOORS

Although the game of **DOORS** is a great way for students to practice characterization, it is even more powerful in forcing students to adapt to unknown situations and environments. The stage is set with two students, one on each side. The area surrounding them becomes an imaginary room that each inhabits. These two rooms are accessed by imaginary doors that reside at the end of a hall that runs from the audience through the middle of the stage.

A third student walks down the hall, opens the door on the right and enters. The occupant immediately involves the student in some sort of activity (singing lessons, buying shoes, group therapy). The new arrival must instantly become part of the scene, never denying what the occupant offers. But within 30 seconds, the new arrival must create a valid reason to leave the room. At the right moment, he opens the door he entered and exits. He then crosses the hall and enters the room on the left. The occupant of this room involves the new arrival in a completely different activity. The difference in the left room is that the occupant must find a valid reason to leave the room. An excuse is stated and the occupant exits in any manner that justifies the excuse. The new arrival now becomes the occupant of the room.

Another student walks down the hall. This time, the first room she will enter will be the left room. Within 30 seconds, she will justify an exit and enter the right room. The occupant will find a reason to exit and make the new arrival the new occupant. This sequence defines the way the game will continue.

Hint...

Set up: One student takes his place in the left room, another in the right room (see top center photo).
Rules for the new arrivals:
Student 1 (photos 1-3)
          Enters Right Room, then exits
          Enters Left Room, the occupant exits
Student 2 (photos 4-6)
          Enters Left Room, then exits
          Enters Right Room, the occupant exits
Student 3 (refer to photos 1-3)
          Enters Right Room, then exits
          Enters Left Room, the occupant exits

Refer to:
Give and Take, Add-a-Scene, Taxi, All Improv games

Hallway

1.

2.

3.

4.

5.

6.

51

HEY, TAXI!

HEY, TAXI! is the most requested game by students who are familiar with improvisational games. With four chairs arranged on stage in "car style" (two in front, two in back), a taxi driver enters the car by opening the door. (Pantomime skills will be severely tested in this activity.) She starts the car and drives off. Soon a "fare" appears off to the driver's right—the passenger side (this would put the fare on the sidewalk, at least in America). The fare hails the cab with the words, "Hey, Taxi!" The driver stops the car (cue brake sound effects), and the "fare" enters the front seat of the car. Please note that anyone entering or exiting the car bears the responsibility of opening and closing the doors! And don't forget your seat belt!

When the passenger sits down, it is up to him to portray a character. This character can be practically anything—an emotion, an animal, an odd physical trait, a funny voice, an occupation, a famous person. As the passenger acts out the character, the driver must discern the traits of the character and immediately act in the same manner.

Within 20 seconds, a second passenger appears and says, "Hey, Taxi!" The driver stops and the new "fare" enters the back seat acting in a way that is totally different from and in contrast to the first passenger. The two in the front seat then take on the trait of the new passenger. A third "fare" appears and enters the back again from the passenger side of the taxi, causing the other person in the back to scoot over behind the driver. A new character is portrayed, and now the other three in the cab emulate the new passenger.

With the taxi now full, a rotation system comes into play. The next passenger hails the taxi and enters the front seat with the driver exiting on the driver's side and the front passenger now becoming the driver. The next passenger then enters the back seat as players continually move to their left when a new passenger enters the taxi.

Hints...

*To apply HEY, TAXI! to your curriculum, have students that enter the taxi portray something from recent studies. To portray Abe Lincoln or a volcano, students will have to use what information they know about whatever they portray.

*To control what content is portrayed in the cab, work up a series of note cards that relay the items that you want the students to characterize. It will still be improv to them!

Refer to:
Give and Take, Contagious Emotion, Freeze, Reruns

"Hey, Taxi!"

"I'm freezin' ..."

"Hey, Taxi!"

"BOC!"

"BOC!"

"BOC!"

A Sound Hint...

When stopping the taxi, the driver uses sound effects to simulate the squeal of the wheels. A good physics lesson comes from how passengers should move when the brakes are applied. Do they lean forward or backward? Ah, inertia...

THE IMPROV GAMES

Note to the Teacher

It is difficult to express the fun of improvisation through mere words. Improv must be experienced to be fully appreciated and understood. The games described on the following pages are a means to that end, representing a plethora of classroom-ready activities that will energize you, your curriculum and most of all, your students. Not only will improv enhance your students' critical and creative thinking skills, but it will demonstrate for them, in very real terms, just how important self-confidence and good judgment are. Improvisation can impact your clasroom in very positive ways. It is your task to apply these activities in a manner most befitting your class, your style and your need. So remember, "If you're not having fun, you're doing it wrong!"

WHAT ARE YOU DOING?

"Imagination is more important than knowledge."
Albert Einstein

The Parents' Credo is "Do as I say, not as I do." This bromide succinctly describes the rules of the game, **WHAT ARE YOU DOING?** Two students take the stage. Player One initiates the game by pantomiming an action (driving a car). Player Two then asks, "What are you doing?" Player One must reply by verbalizing an activity that is totally unrelated to his pantomimed actions (he may say, "Brushing my teeth."). Player Two immediately starts pantomiming the activity spoken by Player One. Player One then asks, "What are you doing?" and Player Two verbally responds with an activity totally unrelated to the pantomimed activity. Player One then begins pantomiming the activity verbalized by Player Two. The game continues in this alternating manner.

WHAT ARE YOU DOING? is the mental equivalent of patting your head and rubbing your stomach. In disassociating the physical and the verbal, the players must quickly switch from using the right hemisphere (spatial/kinesthetic) to the left hemisphere (verbal) of their brains.

Students need to be aware of some of the advanced rules of **WHAT ARE YOU DOING?** 1) There must be a minimal amount of hesitation after being asked, "What are you doing?" In responding to the question, students should make every effort not to say, "I'm... ("I'm...running in the rain!"). When responding, immediately relate the action ("Running in the rain!"). 2) The repeating of previously spoken words and ideas is frowned upon. 3) There should be no similarity between words and actions.

Hint...
Suggest a theme (main idea) for the players to base their actions upon. The main idea of "The Ocean" would spawn responses relating to the sea ("Swimming with sharks").

Anecdote
A class of gifted second graders were watching a demonstration of the game **WHAT ARE YOU DOING?** The class was then asked to state the rules of the game based upon what they had just witnessed. One boy raised his hand and responded, "Well, first of all, you've got to lie."

Refer to:
Pantomime, Word Wide Web, Just Do It!, Freeze

57

THE
PROFESSOR

Did you know..."The sky is blue because small toasters live in Chicago."? You didn't? Well then, you didn't ask **THE PROFESSOR**! Four students take the stage, standing side-by-side. **THE PROFESSOR** answers questions posed by the audience, one word at a time, remembering to form a complete sentence in the process. Each student responds in sequence and without hesitation with a single word that adds to the sentence. One more thing: the answers don't even have to be correct! A simple yet powerful game.

THE PROFESSOR has many variations. Listed are but a few.

DEAR BLABBY: THE PROFESSOR answers personal questions like "Dear Abby." The answer always starts with a greeting to the asker ("Dear Forlorn...").

JEOPARDY PROFESSOR: Instead of a question, **THE PROFESSOR** is given a one or two word answer. The **JEOPARDY PROFESSOR** is required to come up with the question.

MENTAL MATH PROFESSOR: This version of **THE PROFESSOR** ideally uses five people. The first person gives a number (initially keeping it between 0-9). The second in line states an operation ("plus" or "minus," to start with). The third offers a number, the fourth an operation. This continues until, after a player states a number, the following player says, "Equals." The audience, who has hopefully been following the equation, responds with the answer.

STORY PROFESSOR: A narrative (or any other type of prose or poetry) is created one word at a time by **THE PROFESSOR**.

THE...<u>Fill in the blank</u>: THE PROFESSOR can be altered to answer questions as **THE POLICEMAN, THE ROMAN, THE PLUMBER,** or anything else. Questions and answers should relate to the identity of the character.

HINT...
Once students are comfortable with the game, questions pertaining to areas of study can be posed with the expectation of the correct answer. In this manner, **THE PROFESSOR** is a great way to review information.

Refer to:
Beep, Circle Games, Siamese Scene, Spellmaster

"Professor, why do dogs bark?"

"Dogs"   "bark"   "because"   "they"

"have"   "no"   "fancy"   "clothes."

THE SPELLMASTER

Like **THE PROFESSOR**, **THE SPELLMASTER** demands that students be wide open to the possibilities contained within the structure of spelling and grammar. Four students step forward and become **THE SPELLMASTER**. A nonsense word is created by the audience and given to **THE SPELLMASTER** to spell. (Nonsense words are invented, not remembered. Words from The Lion King or Mary Poppins are not acceptable. Challenge students to sequence odd syllables together to get way-out words—"Gravicky," "Trabombo," "Zanfwee"). The first student in line repeats the word and then the word is spelled one letter at a time, one person at a time. When the spelling is completed, the next person repeats the word. Since the word is totally fabricated, the spelling cannot be challenged, since no dictionary contains the nonsense word. **THE SPELLMASTER** is always correct. Upon completion of the spelling of the word, **THE SPELLMASTER** is then asked to define the word, again answering one word at a time.

Hints...

*Ask students not only for the definition, but also for the word's origin (etymology).
*Have **THE SPELLMASTER** use the nonsense word in a sentence, then define the word according to the context clues.
*Have **THE SPELLMASTER** use the nonsense word in a sentence and challenge the class to define the word according to the context clues.
*Give **THE SPELLMASTER** a "theme" to base the definition on ("I understand that 'Zanfwee' has something to do with outer space...").
*Once students are comfortable with the flow of the game, ask them to spell the nonsense words as best they can relating the sound to the appropriate letter.

And More Hints...

*Remember, Fun First. Once students get the handle on this game, give them actual spelling or vocabulary words to spell and define. Expect proper spellings and definitions.
*Students can be asked to spell real words backwards.
*Divide the class into teams and hold **THE SPELLMASTER** SPELLING BEE.

Refer to:
Beep, Circle Games, Professor, Siamese Scene

"Spellmaster, please spell the word 'reogop' and then define it."

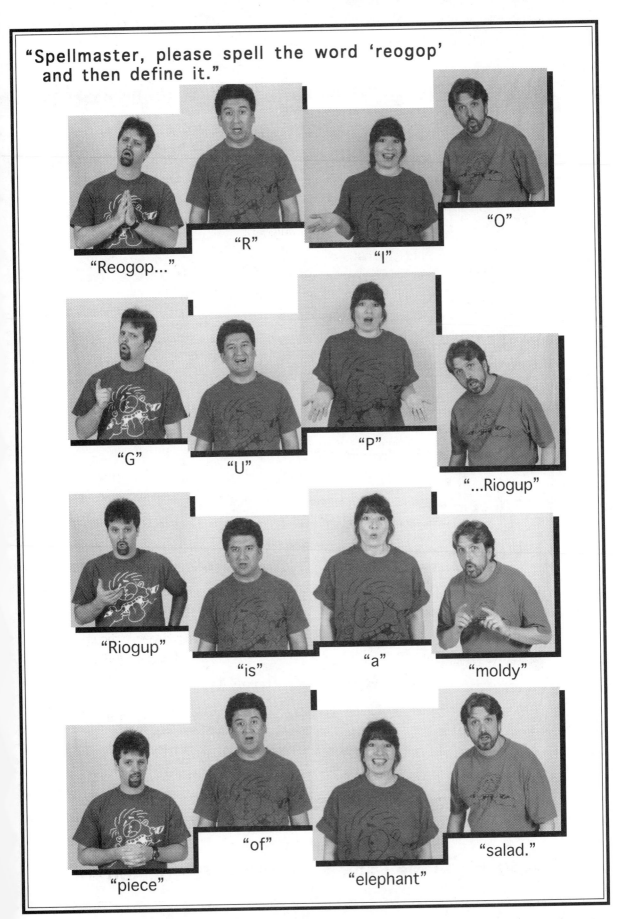

"Reogop..."

"R"

"I"

"O"

"G"

"U"

"P"

"...Riogup"

"Riogup"

"is"

"a"

"moldy"

"piece"

"of"

"elephant"

"salad."

61

STORY
TIME

Five authors. One story. 2000 pounds of fun....

Five students—the authors—take the stage and stand side by side. A story director takes her place by sitting on the floor facing the five. As the director points to an author, that author begins creating a narrative. When the director ceases pointing at the author, he stops, even if in mid-word! The director then selects a different author and that author continues the narrative at the place where the first author left off. During the game, the director switches authors at her discretion and in this manner a story is created. At first the director changes authors slowly. But as the game continues, the director picks up the pace. The authors must pay close attention to both the director and each other as the narrative flows between them **STORY TIME** builds a student's observation skills, creative writing skills and sharpens the memory.

Hints...

*__STORY TIME__ can be applied to more than a narrative. Persuasive, how-to, descriptive and compare/contrast styles of prose can also be adopted.

*As students improve their story telling skills, each author can take on a distinct point of view from which to tell the story. One author could tell his part of the story from the point of view of an "angry" person, another from the point of view of "Abe taxidermist," and still another from the point of view of "Abe Lincoln."

Competitive Hint...

STORY TIME, as a competitive activity, sharpens the skills even further as players do their best not to get called out. The director can call a player out for hesitating, not stopping at the appropriate time or not continuing where the prior player left off.

Refer to:
Letter Point, Circle Games, Taxi, 3-Way Conversation

The title of the story is "The Tiny Whale."

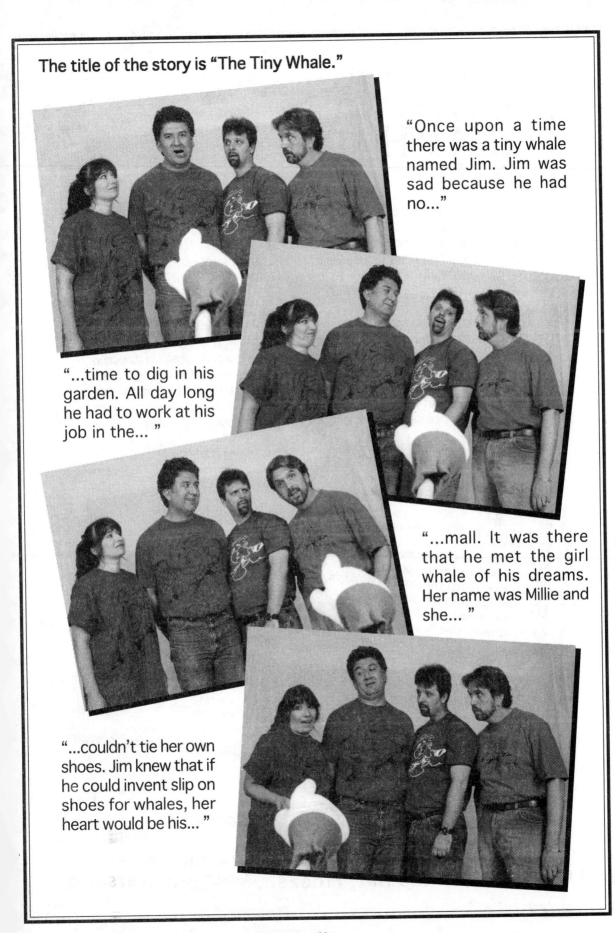

"Once upon a time there was a tiny whale named Jim. Jim was sad because he had no..."

"...time to dig in his garden. All day long he had to work at his job in the... "

"...mall. It was there that he met the girl whale of his dreams. Her name was Millie and she... "

"...couldn't tie her own shoes. Jim knew that if he could invent slip on shoes for whales, her heart would be his... "

MORPH

Situation critical. Apollo 13 astronauts are running out of air. Earth-bound scientists are challenged to reassemble a handful of "square" parts to fit in a round hole or the astronauts will suffocate. They must change the objects to fit a new purpose—in essence, metamorphisizing the objects. The game of **MORPH** demands that students see things as they aren't—to create concrete metaphors.

An object is placed in front of the class. This object can be something familiar or something totally unique (a large cardboard tube). The members of the class must "morph" the object into something other than what it is (the tube changes into a straw for a giant, an elephant trunk, a telescope, a flute). When an idea strikes the mind of the student, she comes to the front of the room and demonstrates (not just tells) the object's new purpose. Students continue to come up and manipulate the object one at a time. Objects are changed out as needed.

Hints...

*Students in the audience attempt to guess the object's new purpose, drawing conclusions from the actions of the actor on stage.

*The object must be "morphed" within the limits of a specific theme (theme: Civil War-The tube becomes a cannon, a sword, a rolled-up document).

*Use two or more objects at the same time.

*Create stories based around the object and its "morphed" purposes. For example, using a large cardboard tube, "Once upon a time, there was a 200 foot gorilla named Cosmo who ran out of toilet paper (the tube is now an empty roll of toilet paper). On his way to the store, he stopped and got a slurpee (the tube is now a huge straw). Suddenly, he realized that he was lost (the tube is now a telescope). He scanned the horizon until he spotted the chimneys of a giant factory (the tube is now a tall smoke stack).

*Challenge students to bring in various items to use in the game.

Refer to:
Clay Play, Give and Take, Justify the Object,
Pass the Hat, Freeze, Just Do It!

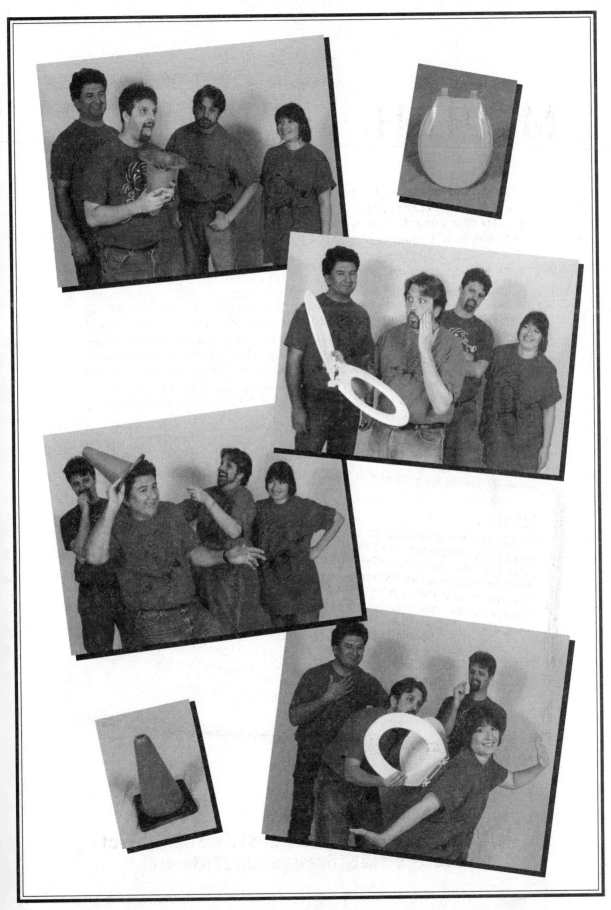

FREEZE!

A student starts pantomiming the action of "swinging a baseball bat."
"Freeze!"
What else does it look like she's doing?

This is the basis for the game, **FREEZE!**. In the front of the room, a student begins pantomiming some everyday activity. "Freeze!" is yelled by the teacher at a critical moment (the height of the action). The class is then asked what other action this frozen form could represent. A volunteer steps to the front of the room, takes the place of the frozen actor and assumes the previous player's exact position. A new activity springs forth from the frozen position. "Freeze!" is yelled again and the new frozen position must be justified by another volunteer. **FREEZE!** must be played BIG! In other words, players must make big movements.

As students' flexibility increases (both mentally and physically), two players may take the stage simultaneously. They are put into an odd-looking position by an audience volunteer. Now, instead of just an action, the two must create a relationship, some dialogue and, hopefully, some sort of conflict. At an advantageous time, "Freeze!" is yelled. An audience member then tags out one of the two frozen actors, assumes the frozen position, and creates a brand new scene using different actions, different characters, and different conflicts. **FREEZE!** expands a student's ability to view a situation from a multitude of perspectives, forcing him to move beyond the obvious while creatively engaging his spatial intelligence.

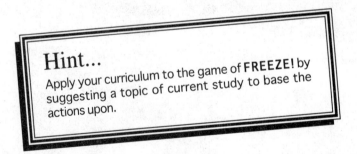

Hint...
Apply your curriculum to the game of **FREEZE!** by suggesting a topic of current study to base the actions upon.

Refer to:
Justify the Object, Pantomime, Give and Take, Doors, Group Stop/Group VCR, Morph

"That's the weirdest fish I've ever seen!"

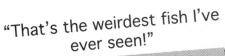

"Here, put it in this net."

"FREEZE!"

"Come on, Ma, it's time to wash the spaghetti."

TAKE ME TO YOUR LEADER

Asking insightful, thought-provoking questions that allow for elaborate responses is an important yet under-developed skill. **TAKE ME TO YOUR LEADER** offers students the opportunity to pose questions to a pair of aliens from a heretofore unknown planet.

Two students are chosen to be the aliens. They must speak gibberish. Two other students are selected to be the interpreters for the aliens. The interpreters act as the linguistic bridge between the audiences' questions and the aliens' responses. The aliens are introduced by the interpreters by name ("This is Meep and Gorno!") and by planet of origin ("They are from the planet Goobix"). The interpreters field the questions from the audience, translate them to the aliens and then interpret the aliens' responses back to the audience.

The set-up of **TAKE ME TO YOUR LEADER** is essential. The audience should be directed to think of questions that pertain to the people, science, social habits, etc. of the planet. The audience should not make assumptions. Cars may not exist on the planet, but transportation does. Football may not be a game in the alien culture, but they probably do have sports.

Lots of Hints...

*Coach the aliens to elaborate upon their answers using gestures and pantomime as an adjunct to their gibberish.

*Coach the audience to ask "fat" questions, questions that don't have "yes" or "no" answers. Short answer questions (How many..., What color...) are also discouraged.

*Follow-up questions can be posed, based upon a previous alien response. This allows for a more detailed approach to the game.

*With the teacher as the interpreter, begin a unit of study (Civil War) with two experts on the subject that are from another planet. Questions posed by the class should be recorded by the teacher, as they are an excellent source of prior knowledge and interest.

*At the end of a unit of study, students play all of the parts in the game. Questions posed by the audience pertain to the unit completed, therefore solidifying their knowledge through a unique form of transfer.

*Turn **TAKE ME TO YOUR LEADER** into a press conference in which the class takes notes on the aliens' responses. A discussion follows the interview in which the facts and details recorded become the basis for inferences one would make about the planet and its inhabitants. (If the atmosphere is made of marshmallow, what can we infer about the inhabitants' modes of transportation or their respiratory systems?) From a few facts and some critical analysis, an elaborate description of the planet can be formulated.

Refer to:
Gibberish, Commercial, Doors, Professor

A question from the audience:
"What do you eat on your planet?"

"Kreyto meeka needtoe
crayneeky?"

"Phrangeegy
zimvwak ena
keemo toopa."

"She says that the
favorite food on their
planet is boiled ice
cream slippers."

(X) WORD SENTENCES

After two players get a topic for a conversation, the audience calls out a number between two and seven (inclusive). The number called out becomes the number of words each sentence will contain—no more, no less. One student starts the conversation using the appropriate number of words. The next student replies with the proper amount of words, and the conversation continues in this manner.

(X) WORD SENTENCES forces the players to be as concise as possible in their verbalizations. Students are immersed in the logic of language, constantly analyzing their thoughts for a correct response. Younger students may approach this game in teams, each team responding to the other (cooperative learning experience). Advanced students may want to adapt the game **SIAMESE SCENE** to **(X) WORD SENTENCES**.

Hints...

*The use of fingers is a natural and acceptable way to count the number of words spoken in a sentence. Encourage the students to be discreet in their counting by holding a hand behind their back or at their side. Eventually, counting will become an internalized process.

*The competitive version of **(X) WORD SENTENCES** allows a player to continue the conversation as long as his sentences conform to the suggested number of words. As soon as a sentence doesn't conform, the player is out. One last comment: O.K. is one word, Okay?

Class Discussion Hint...

Play **(X) WORD SENTENCES** as you carry on a class discussion. Everything spoken must conform to the number of words suggested.

Refer to:
Beep, Reading Warm-ups, Professor, Siamese Scene

RHYME TIME

Two students take the stage and carry on a conversation about a suggested topic as they attempt to rhyme the last phrase spoken by the other player. After the topic of conversation is decided upon (shopping), the first student "feeds" the second student a line ("I went to the store today"). The second student rhymes the line ("Yes, I heard you bought some hay"). The second student then "feeds" a line back to the first student ("Are you going to feed your cow?"). Student number one then rhymes the feeder line ("No, I'll be feeding my sow."), and feeds the second student another line to rhyme. This rhyme/feed pattern continues back and forth. The major objective of the game is to keep the conversation going, not to stump the other person ("I found a cornucopia!" "And I bet you feel like a big dope-ia!").

For the younger student, **RHYME TIME** is a formidable game. It is recommended that the younger participants form teams to respond to one another, either in cooperative groupings (all members of a team work together for the rhyme) or "tag team" matches (any single student who is stumped by a feeder line can trade places with another teammate who has a rhyme). This allows the pace of the game to slow down without diluting the educational benefits of the activity. Advanced students may adapt **RHYME TIME** to specific curricular areas or to appropriate vocabulary words ("Hi, I'm the number nine!" "So, you're not cool; you're not even prime.").

Hints...

Sometimes decisions must be made on the rhymes used. A good example is the "nine"/"prime" rhyme mentioned above. Bring the class into the decision. Use that teachable moment. **RHYME TIME** can be made competitive by forming two opposing teams and disqualifying anyone who cannot rhyme the feeder line. When a student is called "out," the next team member takes the stage. The team with the last player standing is declared the winner. Of course, this makes for a much more difficult game (remember cornucopia?), but it really challenges the students' skills.

Refer to:
Letter Point, Connections, Poetry Corner

CONTAGIOUS EMOTION

"School should be the best party in town."

Peter Kline

CONTAGIOUS EMOTION builds upon the foundation that the game **HEY, TAXI!** establishes. One by one, each character brings a specific emotion or attitude into a scene, and that characteristic is immediately adopted by the other members of the scene.

Each member of a group of three to four students is assigned a different emotion by the members of the audience (contrasting emotions work the best). After receiving the emotions, the group leaves the stage. Player One then re-enters and expresses his suggested emotion through his actions and his dialogue. He does this for 20 to 30 seconds. Upon entering the scene, Player Two portrays his own suggested emotion. Player One immediately switches his emotion to the one portrayed by Player Two. When Player Three enters, they all switch to her emotion, as do they with Player Four. It is important to maintain a contrast between each successive emotion to avoid confusion. (Not: Fear/Anger/Happiness/Silliness, but: Fear/Happiness/Anger/Silliness.)

CONTAGIOUS EMOTION forces players to be totally aware of their actions in relation to their surroundings. It highlights the differences in some emotions, the similarities in others, and the nuances in all. It allows students to practice expressing their feelings in a risk-free environment. Younger students may have a difficult time creating a scene. They may want to pantomime a playground game or some other familiar activity around which to base this game.

Hint...

An easy way to begin a **CONTAGIOUS EMOTION** scene is to have it revolve around a reason for a party. Advanced students may want to reverse the direction of **CONTAGIOUS EMOTION** once the fourth player has entered the scene. They leave the scene in reverse order. Remember that each emotion should take 30 to 45 seconds of scene time before another emotion enters.

Refer to:
Emotional Parade, Bunny, Taxi, Hesitation

RERUNS

RERUNS allows students to perceive a scene from alternating points of view. The audience is told that a group is to perform a short scene and then will replay it a second and a third time using different styles. Students solicit a suggestion from the audience and perform a scene that is appoximately 45 seconds to one minute in length. The scene is devoid of any style. This becomes the "neutral scene" that will be the basis for the replays. The scene should contain a minimum amount of dialogue, since the actors will need to remember it for the replay.

After the scene is completed, the actors give the audience a category or series of categories (emotions, movie styles, animals, music styles, literary genres) and solicit two contrasting styles within those categories. The performers choose which style they will replay first and then repeat their neutral scene, adapting it to the suggested style.

RERUNS brings an acute sense of awareness to actions and words. There is an overwhelming feeling of responsibility for what happens on stage, because everything said and done will be repeated later. **RERUNS** can be adapted to the content areas, whereby different historical figures can replay scenes, or contrasting political views or philosophies can be replayed. (Imagine the signing of the Declaration of Independence by Barney or Hugh Downs.)

Hint...

It is not essential that each replay be a carbon copy of the original. Phrases and actions can be shifted to correspond with the new style. Practice **RERUNS** by staging a short scene, then repeating it verbatim (or as close as the students can come) without first suggesting a new style.

Refer to:
Group Stop/Group VCR, Mirror, 10 Steps

FOREIGN MOVIE

A group of four students is required. Two of the students assume the roles of the "dubbers" whose task it is to speak all of the lines in a scene from off-stage. The remaining two students, the "dubbees," perform all of the physical action of the scene while mouthing the dialogue of the "dubbers," much like a bad Godzilla movie.

After suggestions are solicited, the two "dubbers" take their places at opposite sides of the stage. Each "dubbee" then selects which of the two "dubbers" he will be mouthing. The scene begins as the "dubbees" establish the setting through the use of pantomime. The "dubbers" then begin speaking for their designated "dubbee" as the "dubbees" move their mouths to the words spoken by the "dubbers."

FOREIGN MOVIE allows the shy student to participate with little risk. A student who lacks confidence in speaking in front of a group becomes an excellent "dubbee," while a student who is fearful of the exposure becomes a dynamite "dubber." Younger students enjoy acting out fairy tales or plays read aloud by the teacher or fellow students. In its truest form, though, FOREIGN MOVIE is an interplay between "dubber" and "dubbee." Although the "dubbee" is basically controlled by the "dubber," the "dubbee" is encouraged to physically react in an unexpected manner, causing the "dubber" to have to react to and justify the situation.

Hints...

*You may find that "dubbees" will want to mouth the "dubbers" words exactly as they are spoken. This search for perfection only gets in the way of the game's objective. Remind them that the dubbing does not have to be in perfect sync. Right, Godzilla?

*A brave student gets up in front of the class and becomes the "dubbed" teacher as the actual teacher dubs in the lesson as the student's mouth and movements follow along.

Refer to:
Gibberish, Doors, Taxi, Take Me to Your Leader

"How dare you grow hair on my ship! I'll make you walk the plank!"

"Be careful of what you say, matey. There's a whale selling Rogaine® off the port bow!"

SIAMESE
SCENE

Two players join together to form "Siamese twins," sharing the dialogue and physically acting as a single entity within the context of a scene. SIAMESE SCENE takes a minimum of three people—two to play the twins and a third to be the other character in the scene. The Siamese twins are formed by two students standing close together, each one putting his arm around the other's shoulder or waist. The twins are only allowed to speak as one, each head speaking only one word at a time, going back and forth between the two to present their lines of dialogue. The third actor reacts to the twins as one person, referring to them in the singular. Pantomime skills can be skillfully added to the scene, causing the twins to perform different activities as one (clapping, walking, scratching, jumping rope) during the course of the scene.

SIAMESE SCENE is a cooperative game, working primarily on listening skills, anticipation and sentence formation. The speaking technique used by the twins (back and forth, one word at a time) is applicable to group studies and even cooperative group test taking (two students are asked a test question, and they answer it in Siamese style).

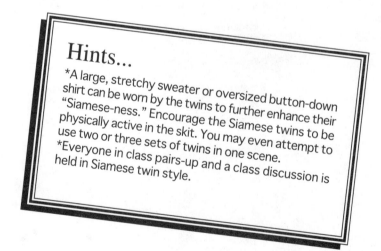

Hints...

*A large, stretchy sweater or oversized button-down shirt can be worn by the twins to further enhance their "Siamese-ness." Encourage the Siamese twins to be physically active in the skit. You may even attempt to use two or three sets of twins in one scene.
*Everyone in class pairs-up and a class discussion is held in Siamese twin style.

Refer to:
Beep, Circle Games, Give and Take, Professor, Spellmaster

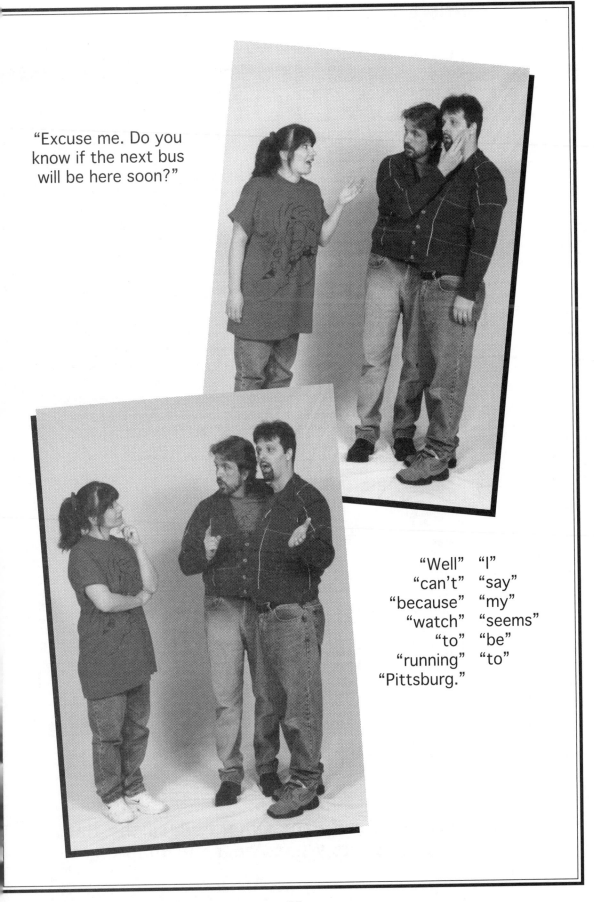

"Excuse me. Do you know if the next bus will be here soon?"

"Well" "I"
"can't" "say"
"because" "my"
"watch" "seems"
"to" "be"
"running" "to"
"Pittsburg."

"To live is to have problems and to solve problems intellectually."

J. P. Guilford

HESITATION

HESITATION incorporates audience suggestions into a scene as it is being played out, forcing the players to justify the suggestions within the context of the scene. The game is played with two to three actors. Once the scene is established, players start hesitating at different points in their dialogues by saying, "Uhh..." ("I went to the store yesterday and bought a Uhh..."). When the audience hears a hesitation, they respond by suggesting a word that would fill in the blank ("Elephant!"). The actor who hesitated must then incorporate the first suggestion he hears into his dialogue. The suggestion, in turn, must be incorporated into the scene ("And boy, was that elephant hard to get out of the store!"). The scene continues with each actor hesitating at pivotal points and the audience responding with a suggestion. The number of hesitations is up to the actors, but it is advised to keep the number low at first to allow total integration of the suggestions into the scene.

HESITATION pumps up the students' problem-solving muscles, the key being how well the suggestions are integrated into the scene. Specific subject areas can be used as hesitation topics. This can result in forced analogy situations, allowing actors and audience alike to see possible connections between heretofore unrelated topics.

Hint...

Since spontaneously expressed audience suggestions are the backbone of this game, you may want to control the way suggestions are solicited. For the full improvisational effect, suggestions are yelled out by the audience and the actors take the first one heard. Since this can result in pandemonium, it may be advisable to have audience members raise their hands to be called on for their suggestions. Audience members may be designated beforehand to respond to the hesitations, thus preventing unnecessary noise pollution. Remind students that the improvisational problem-solving comes from incorporating the suggestions into the scene.

Refer to:
Add-a-Scene, Justify the Object, Pass the Hat, Morph, Doors, What Are You Doing?

POETRY CORNER

POETRY CORNER,
A game of word fun.
Three students step forward
Not four, two, or one.

A topic is given
To students now standing.
Their poem is driven
By the topic. How demanding!

Each student in line
Creates verse one-by-one.
A rhyme would be fine
As long as it's fun.

The pattern of rhyme
Decided at start.
A-A-B-B the first time
Will ease fear in their hearts.

A poem then spoken
From the topic just stated,
Rhyming pattern unbroken,
The players elated!

Pattern two now adopted,
A new topic offered.
A-B-A-B co-opted,
The pattern now tougher.

The poem created,
Sequenced verse by verse
Is immediately related,
Not rambling, but terse.

Pattern three now presented.
Free verse the style.
The topic then rended
but done with a smile!

POETRY CORNER,
A game of fun words.
Students as learners
In a word world absurd.

Refer to:
Letter Point, Rhyme Time,
(X) Word Sentences, Da Do Ron Ron

PUNCH LINE

"Comedy for those who think and a tragedy for those who feel."

Horace Walpole

"Two state representatives walk into a restaurant. The waitress says, 'I'm sorry, we don't serve state representatives here.' And the two state representatives reply, 'That's okay, we don't serve you either!'" This joke was created by an 11-year-old named Brandon. Why, you ask? He was playing the game, **PUNCH LINE**. (By the way, he got big applause.) **PUNCH LINE** uses a standard joke format as the basis for the creation of wonderful (and sometimes horrible) jokes. The format goes like this: "Two _____ walk into a restaurant. The waitress says, 'I'm sorry, we don't serve _____ here.' The two _____ reply, 'Punch Line inserted here.'"

To begin, the audience suggests a noun to serve as the "main idea" for the joke. The players are then obligated to create a punch line based upon the suggestion. When a punch line is developed, the player steps forward and delivers the joke in its entirety. A suggestion is used as long as it's viable. When the suggestion loses its ability to inspire a punch line, a new suggestion is solicited. **PUNCH LINE** emphasizes the creative use of language, focusing primarily on the pun. It encourages divergent thinking in both the players and the audience. Players must find words and concepts associated with the suggestion to create the punch lines. The audience must then "get" the joke, a feat that requires almost as much creativity as creating one.

Hints...

*PUNCH LINE is a game that may require some set up. Initially, have the students brainstorm all of the words that they can come up with relating to an object that they know lots about (books). Ask the students for words from the list that have more than one meaning (page: pages in a book; being paged by someone). Have them create a punch line that incorporates the meaning that does not relate to the topic ("Excuse me, I'm being paged."). From there the students will start to make the "punny" connections needed to play PUNCH LINE.

*Once students are familiar with the game (remember, Fun First!), start applying your curriculum (two pyramids, two atoms, two Titanics). PUNCH LINE will help students understand and retain information by reinforcing the connections between prior knowledge and new information.

Refer to:
Letter Point, Connections, Give and Take, Syllabuild, Naive Expert

Anecdote I

I was being evaluated during a class that I was teaching. After teaching a lesson on Venn diagrams, I closed with the game, **PUNCH LINE**. Students began popping up, giving their instantly-created jokes: "Two Venn diagrams walked in to a restaurant...." Their punch lines reflected many of the concepts and much of the vocabulary they had just learned. After class, the evaluator pulled me aside and, in an accusatory tone, asked me if these jokes had been pre-written. I disarmed her with the facts. Although my students knew how to play the game, **PUNCH LINE**, this was the first time they had ever used "Venn Diagrams" as a suggestion. The evaluator looked down at her forms, scribbled a few notes, looked back up and said with a smile, "Well done."

Anecdote II

A group of visually impaired kids were playing the game **BEEP**. As the beep raced around the circle again and again, a gigantic smile broke out on the face of one young boy as he shouted out, "I can play this game!"

Anecdote III

A large group of fourth graders in a suburban school district were a rather recalcitrant audience, yelling out toward the stage as if the actors were dwelling in the two dimensional world of a big screen TV. Their treatment of the actors was puzzling, if not aggravating. Upon questioning the group as to their behavior during the show, most of the students gazed at the floor in guilt. One boy slowly raised his hand, as if the answer was dawning on him as his arm was being lifted. "Ya' know, you're the first funny adults we've ever seen." Many fourth grade heads nodded in agreement. The frustration harbored toward these students melted into sympathy. "What do you see in adults?" they were asked. Their responses were very revealing.
"Dad hogging the computer."
"Mom constantly on the phone with her clients."
"Dad worried if his clients were self-sufficient."
Their message was clear.

STORY PROBLEM LIVE

"A train heading west at 75 MPH has an engineer named Artie. Artie's watch reads 4:17. If the train travels l.75 hours and Artie's watch is 3 minutes slow, what is the weight of a glazed donut in Moscow when the big hand is on the 12?"

Remember word problems? Remember them? They have been the bane of a teacher's existence due to the negative reaction of students around the world. **STORY PROBLEM LIVE** offers an alternate approach to the read, read, read of word problems. Basically, a group of students acts out an improvised scene in which a main character collects a series of objects that she places in a sack. Different characters enter and exit the scene, "adding" or "subtracting" items from the main characters' sack of stuff. The audience must keep constant track of the number of items as they are added to and taken away from the sack.

Rule Rundown:
1. The main character gets a suggestion from the audience to base the scene on (an occupation, a place, a fairy tale).
2. The audience is made aware of the number of items that exist in the sack prior to the start of the scene. Characters that enter the scene must justify their "additions" or "subtractions."
3. The audience should not use paper or fingers to keep track of number of items.
4. At the end of the activity, students are asked not to yell out the answer. Teachers can get consensus from the class as to the number of items that remain in the sack.
5. Everyone counts together as the number of items left in the sack is revealed.

Hint...
A teacher can introduce this game with a simple acitivity. The teacher walks around the room with a paper sack, first showing the students the number of items that the sack contains As he wanders around the room, conversing with the class and individual students, he puts items from the room in the bag or takes items out and places them back in the classroom environment. The class must keep track of the number of items in the bag.

Refer to:
Add-a-Scene, Fraction Action

DA DO RON RON

Remember the song written by Phil Specter and performed by everyone from the Ronettes to the Carpenters?

Here's a game of Improv where you're gonna sing,
Da Do Ron Ron Ron,
Da Do Ron Ron.
Get yourself a topic and just start to wing,
Da Do Ron Ron Ron,
Da Do Ron Ron.

Yeah, you sing a line,
Another person must make a rhyme,
Then join in on the chorus line.
Da Do Ron Ron Ron,
Da Do Ron Ron.

Make sense? Can't sing? Me neither....
Here's the song applied to a topic of study...

I met him in D.C. that's what I am thinkin',
Da Do Ron Ron Ron,
Da Do Ron Ron.
Somebody said that his name was Lincoln,
Da Do Ron Ron Ron,
Da Don Ron Ron.

Yeah, he was the prez,
"We all are equal," is what he sez.
Emancipation is what he proposed.
Da Do Ron Ron Ron,
Da Do Ron Ron.

Hint...

Before asking students to improvise on a song, have them write the songs out, applying the topic to the song. (No, they don't have to use "Da Do Ron Ron." They can choose a song of their own.)

Refer to:
Syllable Sing, Poetry Corner, (X) Word Sentences

JUST DO IT!

Goethe

JUST DO IT! is similar to Charades, except there is one guesser and a team of clue-givers. The guesser doesn't just sit and watch, but must actually perform the activity in order to guess it. After the guesser leaves the room, the team of clue-givers asks the class for an active activity. Initially, the class should suggest relatively simple tasks (fishing, bowling) in which to engage the guesser. The guesser re-enters the room and the clue-givers involve the guesser in the activity. Most of the communication in **JUST DO IT!** occurs through the use of pantomime. In Charades, the clue-givers cannot verbally communicate with the guessers, but in **JUST DO IT!**, the clue-givers can communicate verbally through gibberish. When it looks like the guesser is actually doing the activity, she is asked, "What are you doing?" If the response is incorrect, the clue-givers must find a new way to approach the activity.

Using a single activity is relatively simple, so once students are comfortable with the communication style that this game demands, they can graduate to more challenging activities. A simple active activity (surfing) is embellished with illogical elaborations (surfing on a refrigerator). Now the clue-givers must employ a structure of logic to present it to the guesser. Usually, the clue-givers get the guesser to do the activity and correctly guess it before adding the illogical embellishments. It is up to the guesser to put the elements together. By guessing along the way, it gives immediate feedback to the clue-givers so that they can alter or elaborate accordingly.

JUST DO IT! is a difficult game to master, but it is worth the time and effort. **JUST DO IT!** exercises deductive reasoning skills, as well as the skills of sequencing, cause and effect, main idea, inferencing and drawing conclusions.

Hints...

*You may want to talk through a few examples before actually playing the game. First, solicit an active activity (playing baseball) and an illogical embellishment (playing baseball with a fish instead of a bat). Ask the students what they would do to convey the activity and then what they would do to communicate the other elements of the activity.

*Guessers who are totally lost are the responsibility of the clue-givers. Let the clue-givers work through their ideas, even if that means taking a time-out to privately discuss the situation.

*Here are some good hints on how to embellish an activity: If the activity uses some type of equipment, replace it with something totally bizarre. Where are they doing this activity? With what famous person are they doing it?

Refer to:
Pantomime, Machine, Connections, Gibberish

Our Guessor,
Bob

"So, Bob, what
are you doing?"

"Playing baseball while
brushing my teeth?"

"Right!"

"Use what you know to
make up what you don't."
Kidprov

SYLLABUILD

Someone just ripped a piece of paper...
There's a horse making a noise...
Someone is kneading bread...
What three syllable word do all these actions add up to?
Ripped paper.......tore
Horse noise........neigh
Kneading bread......dough
tore....neigh....dough
tornado!!

Students select a multi-syllable word, break it down to its syllabic components and act out each of the syllables. A guesser (or guessers) must then put the clues together to conclude the identity of the word. **SYLLABUILD** can be played in "Charade" fashion, with clues given in pantomime form or acted out using more than one person and incorporating gibberish into the activity. Any way it is played, **SYLLABUILD** is a great way to reinforce vocabulary, phonics and a divergent way of thinking (what word does this syllable sound like?).

Hint...

SYLLABUILD's cousin, "**CUSTOMER SERVICE**," is a more involved game in which a customer returns an item to a customer service representative without knowing what it is. Throughout the scene, the rep and other characters give clues to the customer returning the item. Prior to starting, the customer leaves the room. The rep asks the audience for an idea of an object to be returned. He then asks for the object to be made of something totally bizarre. He could even ask for the name of the famous person who previously owned the item. When the customer returns, the clues are presented in a specific order: the object, what it is made of and, finally, the identity of the previous owner. During the scene, the customer continues to guess within the course of the conversation. These guesses give feedback to the other players, helping them to direct their clues.

Refer to:
Beep, Pantomime, Connections, Syllable Sing

NAIVE EXPERT

Two "experts" regale the class with the depth of their expertise. The only problem is that these "experts" are totally clueless as to what they are experts in. **NAIVE EXPERT** is a game of inferencing and drawing conclusions. Two students are selected as the "experts" and leave the room. The host of the show asks the class for a noun (chicken) and an unrelated verb (brushing). This is what the two "experts" are experts in (chicken brushing or brushing chickens). The "experts" then re-enter and an in-depth interview ensues, with the host giving clues within the context of the conversation. The host also goes to the audience for comments and questions. These, too, are clue-loaded. The "experts" glibly answer the questions as they slowly infer the topic of their expertise. When either one of the "experts" has an idea as to their area of expertise, he hazards a guess within the context of the conversation. These guesses give both the host and the audience the immediate feedback needed to decide whether to make the clues more obvious or to move on to the next part (see first hint).

Hints...

*It's always good to agree on how the clues will be given before the experts leave. The most efficient system is to do the verb first, then the noun.

*The host needs to "work-over" the experts in the beginning of the game, asking them how they started in this occupation, why they chose this field of endeavor, etc. The host must ask pointed questions in order to pin the experts down, even though they have no idea what that is.

Refer to:
Connections, Commercial, Top That!, Yes, but...

GLOSSARY

Attitude: an emotion, characteristic, occupation, or dialect that a player expresses in a skit (anger, athletic, truck driver, Russian).

Denial: the act of refusing to accept what another player says or does on stage. This is a major sin in Improv.

Establish the Where: the pantomimed movements found in the first few moments of a scene that define for the audience the place that the actors are occupying.

Flow: the continuous give and take in a scene defined by its energy, its fluidity and its creative spiraling.

Focus: the ability of a player to give total attention to his activity, both internally and externally.

Give and Take: the sharing of dialogue and action in a scene by the actors with emphasis on listening and responding.

Improvisation (Improv): the act of creating on the spot by using what is at hand (without preparation).

Justify: to give logical reasons why something is.

Neutral Scene: a scene in which no definable attitudes exist.

Pantomime: the act of communicating through movement.

Scene Game: any game in which actors create a plot through the use of dialogue and pantomime, usually involving a conflict.

Stage: wherever improv is performed (classroom, library, theater).

Suggestion: an idea supplied by an audience member that gives the basis for an improvisational activity.

Warm-up: an activity that reinforces the skills needed to perform improvisational games.

REFERENCES

Baron and Sternberg. (1987). <u>Teaching Thinking Skills</u>. New York: W. H. Freeman and Company.

Csikszentmihalyi, M. (1990). <u>Flow—The Psychology of Optimal Experience</u>. New York: Harper Perennial.

Csikszentmihalyi, M. (1996). <u>Creativity</u>. New York: Harper Collins Publishers.

DeBono, E. (1992). <u>Serious Creativity</u>. New York: Harper Business Press.

Grudin, R. (1990). <u>The Grace of Great Things</u>. New York: Ticknor and Fields.

Koestler, A. (1964). <u>The Act of Creation.</u> London: Penguin Group.

Michalko, M. (1991). <u>Thinkertoys</u>. Berkley: Ten Speed Press.

Mitchley, J. (1982). <u>Five Thousand Years of Theatre</u>. London: Batsford Academic and Educational Ltd.

Nachmanovich, S. (1990). <u>Free Play</u>. New York: Tarcher/Putnam.

Perkins, D. N. (1981). <u>The Mind's Best Work</u>. Cambridge: Harvard University Press.

Priestley, J. B. (1969). <u>The Wonderful World of Theatre</u>. Garden City: Doubleday and Co.

Senge, P. (1990). <u>The Fifth Discipline</u>. New York: Doubleday.

Other Books on Improvisation

Barry-Winters, L. (1997). <u>On Stage: Theater Games and Activities for Kids</u>. Chicago: Chicago Review Press.

Frost, A. (1989). <u>Improvisation in Drama</u>. New York: St. Martin's Press.

Goldberg, A. (1991). <u>Improv Comedy</u>. Hollywood: Samuel French Trade.

Halpern, Close, Johnson. (1994). <u>Truth in Comedy</u>. Colorado Springs: Meriwether Publishing.

Hodgson and Richards. (1974). <u>Improvisation</u>. New York: Random House.

Horn, D. (1991). <u>Comedy Improvisation</u>. Colorado Springs: Meriwether Publishing.

Johnstone, K. (1981). <u>Impro: Improvisation and the Theatre</u>. New York: Routledge.

Novelly, M. (1985). <u>Theatre Games for Young Performers</u>. Colorado Springs: Meriwether Publishing.

Schotz, A. (1998). <u>Theatre Games and Beyond</u>. Colorado Springs: Meriwether Publishing.

Spolin, V. (1983). <u>Improvisation for the Theater</u>. Evanston: Northwestern University Press.

Spolin, V. (1985). <u>Theater Games for Rehearsal</u>. Evanston: Northwestern University Press.

Wiener, D. (1994). <u>Rehearsals for Growth</u>. New York: Norton & Company.

Brad Newton's books:

Improvisation, 2nd Edition

and

Improse (Improvisational Prose)

may be ordered from:

Gifted Psychology Press, Inc.,
P.O. Box 5057
Scottsdale, AZ 85261

Phone: (602) 954-4200
Fax: (602) 954-0185

www.giftedpsychologypress.com

For information about Kidprov, contact:

Brad Newton
1430 Susan Lane
Carrollton, TX 75007

Phone: (972) 394-8245

www.kidprov.com